Transition
From Forgotten to Forgiven and Highly Favored

Naleighna Kai

The Macro Group, LLC
Chicago, Illinois

This book is a work of nonfiction. These accounts are from the author's perspective and memories, and as such, are represented as accurately and faithfully as possible. To maintain the anonymity of the individuals involved, some of the names and details have been changed.

Transition: From Forgotten to Forgiven and Highly Favored
Copyright © 2021 by The Macro Group, LLC All rights reserved.

Edited by Janice M. Allen and
J. L. Campbell: jlcampbellwrites@gmail.com
Cover Designed by J. L Woodson: www.woodsoncreativestudio.com
Interior Designed by Lissa Woodson: www.naleighnakai.com
Beta Readers: D. J. Mitchell and Kelsie Maxwell

ISBN 978-1-952871-13-9 (trade paperback)
ISBN 978-1-952871-14-6 (E-Book)

Without limiting the rights under copyright reserved above, no part of this publication may be reproduced, stored in, or introduced into a retrieval system, or transmitted, in any form, or by any means (electronic, mechanical, photocopying, recording, or otherwise) without the express written permission of both the copyright owner and the publisher of this book, except in the case of brief quotations embodied in critical articles and reviews. The scanning, uploading, and distribution of this book via the Internet or via any other means without the permission of the owner is illegal and punishable by law. For permission, contact Naleighna Kai at naleighnakai@gmail.com.

The Macro Group, LLC
1507 E. 53rd Street, #858
Chicago, IL 60615

Scripture quotations are taken from the King James Version (KJV), public domain.

Transition

From Forgotten to Forgiven and Highly Favored

Naleighna Kai

DEDICATION

Jean Woodson,
Eric Harold Spears,
LaKecia Janise Woodson,
Mildred E. Williams,
Anthony Johnson,
L. A. Banks,
Octavia Butler,
Tanishia Pearson Jones,
Emmanuel McDavid, and
Priscilla Jackson

J. L. Woodson & Donisha
Shawn Williams, Sesvalah, Ehryck,
La Ammitai, Jamyi Joi, Janine Ingram, and the
members of NK's Tribe Called Success

ACKNOWLEDGEMENTS

Special thanks goes out to: The Creator from whom all Blessings and opportunities flow, Sandy (my true mother), my son, J. L. Woodson (for the awesome cover designs for this Merry Hearts series), Sesvalah, Bettye Odom, Janice M. Allen, Debra J. Mitchell, Royce Slade Morton, Bunny Ervin, J. L. Campbell, Kelly Peterson, Janine A. Ingram, Ehryck F. Gilmore, Betty Clawson, Jamyi Joy, Stephanie M. Freeman, Unique Hiram, Marie L. McKenzie, Shawn Williams, Dr. Vanessa Howard, the Kings of the Castle Ambassadors, Members of Naleighna Kai's Literary Cafe, the members of NK's Tribe Called Success, the members of Namakir Tribe, and to you, my dear readers . . . thank you all for your support.

Much love, peace, and joy,
Naleighna Kai

Naleighna Kai

She is a phoenix rising from the ruins of her despair. Her garment greets the wind like an old friend, honoring the bravery, marveling at the miles. Forever forward she moves; every footfall paves the way for the ones that follow. Past, present, and future ripple and writhe beneath the fabric of her existence. The storms of her past are swallowed whole as passion and purpose swirls her.

Using her pen as a sword, the determined one slays the darkness. Words that flow from her heart to the page sing of home and safe haven for those still lost in the storms.

—Stephanie M. Freeman, author of Necessary Evil, Unfinished Business, and Nature of the Beast

Introduction

The Merry Hearts Inspirational Series and this particular book taught me about being open, flexible, and understanding it's all about growth. NK's Tribe Called Success has done a number of series centered around romantic suspense, and it left our inspirational fiction authors on the sidelines. So I had to be flexible.

Instagram started as a regional app called Burbn that focused on the developer's love of fine whiskeys and bourbon. Back then, it simply allowed users to check-in, post their plans, and share photos. When he saw that the app kept expanding beyond what he imagined, he didn't dig in his heels and say, "No, it has to stay within the vision I wanted. They have to use it the way it was created." He listened to what the users wanted, grew from there, and look where the app is today.

The same thing happened with Merry Hearts. I kept putting it on the back burner because all the other genres absorbed my time. Then because of a new audio-only app, I started a 30-day challenge and helped several women who wanted to bring their life stories and self-help books and into the light. Some started in late January, others in the latter part of February and they, who had never written a book before, released their first books in June with the support of my entire writing tribe. All four books, back to back, became #1 Amazon Bestsellers and stayed number one for several days, not just hours.

Still, my focus was on the next series to come—the Queens of the Castle. Until ... I slid into a room on the app and Shawn Williams, a prophetess, brought me on the stage. She read me up and down for not doing what The Creator called me to do—write an inspirational series with the Tribe that would inspire people when they truly needed it, at this moment, in these interesting times. She was right. Even in the writing process, several authors shared dark parts of their past that they hadn't told anyone. We began working toward the finish line, but prayed for each other as the tears came and the healing began.

This would never have happened if I didn't expand my vision beyond only working with authors who write fiction, romance, science fiction, mysteries, and thrillers, to actually realize that I could help people who simply wanted to tell their truth in a manner that would also help my writing tribe.

What I learned from this experience, is that I have to be open to manifestation coming in ways that are best for the Universe, ourselves, and everyone involved. And when I'm on the phone with an author who is seeing their cover for the first time, it brings me such joy to know that I was the vessel through which their dream happened. This is so simple to me but means the absolute world to them.

It is my hope this series will touch your heart and mind in exactly the way you need.

Each book in the Merry Hearts Series is a standalone and can be read in any order:

Book 1 – Journey – Lisa Dodson [Ruth and Boaz]
Book 2 – Vision – J. L. Campbell [The Outside Child]
Book 3 – Purpose – Florenza Denise Lee [The Unnamed Woman]
Book 4 – Growth - Janice Allen [Esther and The Three Hebrew Boys]
Book 5 – Transition—Naleighna Kai [The Levite's Concubine]
Book 6 – Choices – Pat G'Orge-Walker [The Faithful Wife]
Book 7 – Patience – Terri Ann Johnson [Moses]
Book 8 – Persistence – U. M. Hiram [Hannah, The Centurion]
Book 9 – Transformation – Naleighna Kai [Tamar and Amnon]

Chapter 1

The Runaway Bride

*And it came to pass in those days, when there was no king in Israel
…—Judges 19:1*

"You need to come home now," the Levite demanded. "It's been four months since you left Ephraim."

"I'm not ready to leave my father's house," she said, moving away from the threshold until she stood behind her father, as though he could protect her from the consequences of what she had done. "There's nothing but death for me back there."

The Levite moved sideways and extended his hand to her, saying, "Come home."

She refused to budge. Instead, she pulled her robe about a frame that was much more slender than it had been several days ago.

Her father stepped between them and said, "Why don't you stay for the night and let's talk about things?"

The Levite sighed. This trip to Bethlehem was causing him as much grief as his concubine had four months ago, when she was out having a good time with men who had no legal right to any part of her. After being found in a compromising position, she ran away to the relative safety of her father's home. Something that was unheard of in this day and time. The Levite would have been well within his rights if he had chosen to have her stoned. He shelved that thought—for now—and resigned himself to staying.

Four days in a row, his father-in-law had "encouraged" him to spend yet another night. The Levite stayed far longer than he'd intended, as the patriarch tried to make sure things were going to be all right with his daughter and that all had been truly forgiven.

On the afternoon of day five, the Levite held firm to his conviction. Without further delay he would return to his homeland with his concubine. He had to teach on Saturday, and he'd been gone from his congregation long enough. After reassuring his father-in-law that his daughter would be safe, they set out on their journey.

Nightfall was approaching when they arrived near a Jebusite city. Unfortunately, they were still nowhere near close to home. The Levite raised his hand to halt their progression on the dusty road.

His servant came forward, nearly stumbling from weariness. "We should find someplace to stay in this city."

"I don't want to stay here," the Levite snapped, scrunching up his nose as though he smelled something rotten. "They are not of Israel." He lifted his chin and said, "We're going to Gibeah, instead."

"Do you have friends in that area?" the concubine asked, pulling her garment about her to fight off the nighttime chill.

He slid a gaze her way. "No, but we'll be all right."

"By traveling another several hours to Gibeah?" she shot back, causing the servant to nod his agreement.

"I'm tired and hungry," the Levite said with a resigned sigh.

"Wouldn't be that way if you had listened to my father and stayed one more night."

He gave her a dismissive wave. "We had stayed long enough. And we wouldn't have been there in the first place if ..."

She tilted her head, almost daring him to finish his statement. The argument should have been a moot point anyway because of the Jewish law of forgiveness.

The servant pulled the donkey up short. "You're choosing Gibeah over Jebus because it's supposed to be safer?"

"Those Jebus people aren't who we should associate with. So, we're going to—"

"Gibeah?" the servant confirmed, his dark-brown gaze narrowing to slits.

"Why does everyone keep asking that?" he asked trying to keep the anger from his voice. "I said it already. Twice. Shall we?" He gestured for the servant to move. "We will be fine in Gibeah."

"Famous last words," the servant said under his breath.

The Levite and his party continued on. Traveling in the arid weather had left the trio parched, exhausted, and famished. His concubine and servant would thank him when one of the residents of Gibeah offered to provide food and water for them and their donkey, as well as lodging for the night. Travelers could expect this customary hospitality from fellow Israelites, even if they were complete strangers.

Reaching Gibeah, they waited in the market located squarely in the center of the city.

No one so much as gave them a second look, let alone offered them a place to stay.

Eventually, an old man came in from working in the field and asked, "So what brings you around these parts?" He wore a garment made of sheep's wool that dwarfed his fragile frame.

The Levite glanced at his concubine and said, "Well, she took it upon herself to have a vacation without me."

"She ran home to her father's place?" The old man's eyes widened to the size of platters.

The servant came close to snickering.

"Something like that," the Levite mumbled, angered at the reminder that traveling merchants brought more than their wares to their destinations. They readily spread any news—good or bad—they learned along the way. The woman, leaving the way she did, had embarrassed him to an eternal degree. Now he'd have to live with the aftermath when they made it home. At least, she hadn't run to a lover for protection. Then he wouldn't have been able to intervene in her fate. His anger wouldn't have allowed it. Her father speaking up for her was another thing entirely. And extracting the Levite's promise to forgive her allowed her to remain alive.

"No worries," the host said, as though sensing the discomfort his observation had caused. "I am also from the mountains of Ephraim, but I've lived here among the Benjamites for some time now. We need to get you out of the public square and into my place right away."

"We don't want to impose," The Levite said, though inwardly he was relieved at the offer.

"Nonsense." The old man gestured for them to follow him. "You can't stay here in the open. We will have a great meal, some good music, and in the morning you'll be on your way."

The servant and the concubine exchanged a glance as their master answered the host with, "Sounds like a plan."

Chapter 2

Home Sweet Home

The host brought them to a modest abode quite a ways from the public square. He gave fodder to the donkeys and put them in a small stable. Before they crossed the threshold, he provided a basin of fresh water for his guests to wash their feet.

His place was a single-story home, simple and modest, with a rough stone foundation and mudbricks, plus a small amount of wood.

"Put her with the other women," the host commanded his wife, shooing the concubine toward the rear of the room where weaving materials were stacked against a wall. The servant followed the host's manservant to another area.

The concubine flinched, then glared at her husband, who tried to ignore that look she and the servant exchanged. When she was out of earshot and engaged in conversation with the other women, the host asked, "Wife or concubine?"

Fair question, since having a concubine was a lower form of marriage. Still respectable, but not as legal as a wife. Either way, she was still his property. She'd been raised in a family-centered agrarian society in Bethlehem, and he had secured her as a pilegesh—a lower level wife who was beholden only to him, and who was there for his pleasure and use. Somehow, she hadn't gotten that memo or the scroll that it was scribbled on.

"Concubine," he answered, seething at the fact that if she had not taken it upon herself to run, he would not be bone weary right now. He'd be at home, comfortable in his own bed, not at the mercy of someone else's hospitality. "Her father tried to keep me from leaving because he felt so honored to have me there."

"Honored?" the host asked, taking a sip of red wine from a goblet.

"As a priest, they kind of consider me royalty," he replied. "She did me wrong, then when she was found out, she ran away to avoid the consequences."

The host shook his head, chuckling as he added, "Stoning is still a thing, yes?"

"Indeed, but I chose to speak kindly to her, showing her mercy and forgiveness," he said, taking a bite of lentil stew. "I was more than ready to come home once her father was finally reassured that all would be well between us, and—"

A sharp rap on the door caught everyone off guard. The host looked to his servant, who was in the act of placing a platter of barley bread in the center of the table.

"Isn't everyone already home?" the host asked.

"Yes, sir, everyone knows to make it inside before dark."

"Then who is that knocking on the door?" His gaze slid toward his wife, who left the meal being shared by the women.

After peering through the window, she answered, "Several men from town. They've surrounded the house."

"Ignore them," her husband said, "we're feasting." The flourish of his hand signaled for everyone to resume their meal.

The banging resumed, this time much louder, and drowned every other sound in the home.

"Bring out the man who came to your house," they cried. "That we may know him."

"Enough of this," the host roared as he stormed from the table. Snatching open the door, he was met by a host of men on the other side. "What do you want? We're having supper."

"You know what we want," one of the tallest men said with a slight waver in his steps as if he'd already had one goblet of wine too many. "We'd like to join the party."

The homeowner squared his shoulders. "We don't have enough to feed all of you."

"Then we can party out here with the traveler," another one said, clasping the shoulder of the man standing directly in front of him. "We don't need food. Just send him out."

"We don't have anything to worry about," the Levite whispered to his concubine, who inched closer to him. "The law of hospitality means we are protected."

She grimaced, as if she didn't believe a word. The action matched those of the other two women standing nearby.

"Bring him out," the drunken horde chanted.

"The crowd is growing larger," the host's wife said with another anxious look out of the window. "This can't be good."

The host thought that over for a few moments as the shouts and ire of the crowd amped up to a more dangerous level. "I have a solution ..." he said, connecting a pointed gaze with his wife.

Judging by the woman's crestfallen expression, the Levite guessed that she knew exactly what that solution entailed. Fighting them wasn't even on the table. Sheer numbers, combined with the host's age, ruled that out. And the male servants he'd seen around the host's home didn't rate as a sacrifice. No, one or more of the women in the house would be offered to the crowd outside the door. Allowing them to violate the women would be less ... shameful than violating his male guest, which would be an attack on not only his body but his honor as well.

"My virgin daughter and my guest's concubine," the old man continued. "Have at them. Do whatever you like."

A stocky man pushed his way through the crowd and said, "We don't want them, we want —"

The debate went on for several minutes, but nothing dissuaded them. Finally, the Levite pushed his concubine toward the threshold.

"Is this the act of a man who has truly forgiven my trespasses?" she shrieked, struggling to get past him to the safety of the back of the house.

"I did forgive you," the Levite countered. "But it isn't like you're unfamiliar with accepting other men inside your body or your bed, soooo..." He winked. "Better you than me."

With the help of the homeowner, he thrust her into the arms of the waiting men. The door slammed after her, and the Levite and host went back to their meal.

Following their lead, everyone in the house ignored her screams for help and continued what they'd been doing before the crowd appeared.

Chapter 3

What's Done in the Dark

The sun struck a strange bargain with the morning sky, rising to shed light on the horrific activities the night before. The men had used and abused her all night, not letting her go until dawn. She had collapsed outside the door, one bloody hand splayed across the threshold.

The Levite had a breakfast of roasted grain, figs, and bread dipped in olive oil, then bid the host and his family farewell.

He stretched, then cracked his neck to both sides, ignored the glare from his servant, and made his way to the door. When he tried to step over the threshold, he was met by the familiar form stretched out on the ground.

"Get up, and let's go," he said through his teeth, irritated by the sight of her and the reminder that if he hadn't taken her father up on those offers to tarry, they would have been home days ago.

The silence from the concubine, along with the fact that she didn't move, added just a smidgen of alarm to the Levite's growing exasperation.

"Oh, come on," he quipped, nudging her with his sandal. "It couldn't be that bad."

Still no movement.

Fear stabbed the center of his heart. How would he explain this? He had promised her father that everything would be fine and all was forgiven, and now this happened.

Resigned to the horrendous outcome, he picked her up and tossed her over the back of the donkey, realizing he could never mention to anyone that he had handed her over to those men to save himself.

* * *

The Levite's home was situated in a hilly region and made of whitewashed bricks. A larger room in front served the purpose of living and dining areas, with quarters in the back of the home for sleeping and servants. The much smaller back room was set aside for the animals and their care.

He had sent everyone away before stretching the concubine's body out on the wooden table. "How on earth do I explain to everyone what happened to her?" he whispered, despite the fact that he was alone.

Maybe, he could simply bury her and say she expired on the ride home. But her father wouldn't believe a word of it. Besides, the servant and their host knew the true story. A week ago, all he had to worry about was who his concubine was sleeping with. He never had to worry about any of that again. She was with her Maker, and he was left to clean up the mess she made.

"Let's see. Twelve tribes. Maybe a note?" he mused. If he made sure everyone else was pissed off at what the other men did to her, then they wouldn't be pointing the finger at him.

As soon as he made the decision, he selected a knife and held it above her body for a few minutes. Every possible warning bell went off in his mind. What he planned to do was against God's law. *Do not defile a corpse.* Doing so would mean that even in death, he refused to let his concubine have any dignity.

The Levite gathered whatever strength he had and carved her body into twelve pieces, preparing to send one to all the coasts of Israel.

Holding a parchment made of animal skins, he prepared to etch a message. Maybe he should mention that she had been handed over because he had no choice.

"No, they don't need to know that part," he whispered. *Just a tiny lie of omission.*

The first words he wrote were, "Look at what these Benjamites have done to my concubine."

***

Filled with outrage, the men from all the tribes convened at a place called Mizpah within days. The leaders of the tribes, along with 400,000 foot soldiers, presented themselves before the congregation of men. Spotting the Levite, one of the elders beckoned for him to join them at the front of the gathering.

Making his way through the crowd, the Levite overheard comments from a few of the men.

"Did you see what those Benjamites did?" one man asked a member of a neighboring tribe as they waited in the open, under the blazing sun.

"What part did you all get?"

"Hard to miss an entire arm landing on your doorstep," came the dry reply.

"Could've just sent a note," another grumbled over his shoulder.

"I did," the Levite shot back, glaring at the men, who promptly found a pointed interest in their garments.

One of them shrugged. "I mean just a note, without all the theatrics and whatnot."

"Well, you got my message, didn't you?" he snapped, angered that his intended dispatch was getting lost in translation. He scanned the faces of the men at the assembly, which were all etched with varying expressions of impatience, anxiety, and anger. "What are you all going to do?" he demanded. "No one's going home until we figure this out."

"Thank God we have tents," someone mumbled.

"Won't be going there, either," the Levite shot back.

The eldest man from one of the largest tribes stood and said, "All I know is that from this day forward, none of us shall give his daughter to a Benjaminite as a wife."

A roar of approval went up from all tribes who also chimed in on that vow. When the clamor finally died down, another one added, "They must turn over the men who did this."

Those words were also met with confirmation from every man in attendance.

"You know, before we do something drastic," Messiah, a man from the tribe of Asher said. "Let's send them a message and give them a chance to do the right thing."

"We don't need to do that," another answered. "We can't be associated with that kind of behavior."

In the end, they sent men to the tribe of Benjamin, demanding that they hand over the men who were involved in the crime so they could be executed.

* * *

Without waiting for the messenger to catch his breath, one of the leaders of the tribes asked, "What was their answer?"

"In a word—no," the messenger answered, nearly out of

breath from the long journey. "They'd rather go to war to protect those criminals in Gibeah."

"Well if it's war they want, it's war they'll get," one of the men further in the back said. "Let's kill them all."

The overwhelming response was in the affirmative.

Messiah stood, waving his arms to get everyone's attention. "I don't want to be the voice of dissension here, but don't you think we should talk to God first?"

Some paused, but several men waved away that thought as the more vocal ones in the group said, "We've got this. No need to bother God for a little skirmish between tribes."

"He's right," an elder said. "Let's go before God and let Him know our plans and get some direction."

"I think you got that backward," Messiah shouted. "You're supposed to ask God what we should do, not tell Him what we're going to do."

"We're going to war," the man said, glowering at Messiah. "We just need to know how."

"Or you're going at it like this because you're afraid God will tell you that you shouldn't battle these people at all."

His words sent silence through the camp, but only for a moment.

Chapter 4

Onward Christian Soldiers

Good sense prevailed, and the tribes asked God if they should go to war. The first time they asked, God said to send the Tribe of Judah into battle. Evidently, that was all the affirmative response they needed.

The rebels defending Gibeah numbered 26,000, 700 of whom were left-handed and could sling a stone at something as small as a hair on a man's head without missing the target.

On the first day of battle, the Israelites suffered more loss than they thought possible. Day two was more of the same.

"How is it we outnumber them and they're kicking our behinds?" one who had been on the frontline asked as they sat in camp around that fire that evening.

Messiah shrugged, knowing that speaking his thoughts was almost always met with derision.

The war continued, and after getting their tailbones—and other parts—handed to them, the combined forces finally went to the house of God to have another little chat.

They sat before the Lord, where the Ark of the Covenant resided, and didn't eat anything until later that day. They took things a step further by offering up a few burnt offerings and peace offerings before the Lord.

Thankfully, they received an affirmative answer: "Go up, for tomorrow I will deliver them into your hand."

The combined forces set a trap, and when they appeared to be retreating, the Benjamites were hot on their trail, sensing weakness and victory. Little did they know, the rest of the Israelites hid and were lying in wait.

A cloud of smoke went up as a signal, and the remainder of the combined forced rushed in. When the Benjamites saw their city in flames and realized that the Israelites had played them, they ran to the desert.

The Israelites were on them like white on sheep's wool.

Only six hundred of them survived, and that was because they were hiding out in Rimmon. The Israelites retreated, went back through all the towns and cities of the Benjamites and destroyed everyone and everything—women, children, men, and even the livestock. All because the Tribe of Benjamin wouldn't give up one small group of criminals.

* * *

Celebrations were in high gear in the camp that evening, with the men eating, drinking, and jesting.

Messiah stood and raised his hand, and the voices reluctantly trickled to a halt. "So, now we have another problem."

"Why are you always the bearer of bad news?" someone mumbled.

"Because you all rush in without getting good consult from

God," he countered. "First of all, vengeance is mine saith the Lord."

"Well, we did have things under control," someone shot back.

Messiah stood and shook a hand at them. "No, you had to go in to have a talk with God after you'd already messed up by making a decision, then asking Him to cosign on what you'd already set your mind to do. You all were so sure you would wipe them out with no problem whatsoever. Guess they showed you, didn't they?"

Grumbles of dissent echoed. "Now what's this problem you spoke of?"

"He's talking about the fact that we are in danger of losing an entire tribe," a member of the Tribe of Simeon said. "There's only six hundred of them left."

"Didn't realize the war was going to be so effective," one from the tribe of Dan asserted.

"It was eleven tribes to one," Messiah protested with a fierce glare. "What did you think was going to happen?"

Silence reigned for several moments as a few of them shifted under the weight of that observation.

"So, what are we going to do?"

"They can replenish themselves," a member of the tribe of Reuben said. "The six hundred men who slipped through our fingers and got away during the battle will surely go back to rebuild Gibeah when they think the threat is over."

"Exactly how are they going to replenish themselves?" Messiah asked, smirking and shaking his head. "You killed all the women and children. All of them."

A panic-stricken expression fell over the faces of several elders. "Well, we already vowed that our daughters could not marry them, so that's going to add to the problem."

"If they can't marry," an elder from the Tribe of Judah said, bushy eyebrows furrowing as he ran a hand over the whisper-thin hair on his head. "And they don't have any women of their own …"

Messiah put a hand on his hip and said, "And you're just thinking of this—"

"Will you shut up?" a silver-haired man from the Tribe of Issachar snapped. "We get it already."

"From your lips to God's ear."

The gathering was silent for a long while. All elation at having been victorious in the war was overshadowed because their covenant with God required them to have twelve tribes at all times.

Finally, someone spoke up. "Well, none of the men from Jabesh Gilead area came to the first meeting, so they're fair game. We should kill them all, plus the women and children, and only leave the virgins alive. We can take *them* to the Benjamite men."

Messiah raised his hand a second time. "So, they decided to stay out of this mess you made, and you're going to punish them by killing them off, taking their virgins, and giving them to the very people you been decimating these past few weeks? Is that what I'm hearing?"

"We have to do something," an elder from the Tribe of Ephraim mumbled.

"Didn't you learn anything from that battle with the Benjamites?" Messiah asked, eyeing the men as though they were rebellious children. "Once again, you're just going to make up your own minds. Then you'll go running off to war without consulting God about what we should do first, instead of telling him what you're going to do and asking His input like the first time."

An elder from the Tribe of Dan gave a dismissive wave.

Messiah glared at him until the man mumbled under his breath, "Shouldn't we consult God first?"

Transition: From Forgotten to Forgiven and Highly Favored

***

The combined forces of Israel sent twelve thousand men into Jabesh Gilead to kill all the inhabitants, except the virgins. They gained four hundred young virgins for their efforts and brought them to a camp at Shiloh, in the land of Canaan.

"So, we have four hundred virgins, and we're still two hundred short," an elder from the tribe of Zebulun boasted.

"At least math is your strong suit," Messiah snarled.

A collective groan went up from everyone, along with a few side eyes at him.

The elders conferred for a few moments, then came back with, "Go and tell those knucklehead Benjamites that we have some women for them. And that we come in peace."

***

The Benjamites received the message and arrived at the camp of the combined forces, who presented them with the women whom they had captured in Jabesh Gilead. The women huddled together in groups, frightened as they awaited their fate.

"Six hundred of us, four hundred virgins," one of the Benjamites said in a dry tone.

Messiah placed a finger across his lips as though to silence the thought that came to mind, but couldn't help himself. "Their math is pretty good too."

"Where's the fun in that?" another Benjamite piped up. "What do you expect us to do, practice polyandry?"

A thunderous roar of dissent rose up at the thought of something as abhorrent as a woman being shared by two men. It simply was not done.

And the people grieved for Benjamin, because the Lord had made a void in the tribes of Israel. Well, to be honest, *they* had caused said void, but who was keeping track of all that?

Then the elders of the congregation asked, "What shall we do for wives for those who remain, since the women of Benjamin have been destroyed?"

And they also said, "There must be an inheritance for the survivors of Benjamin, that a tribe may not be destroyed from Israel."

"Couldn't we just ..."

"No, we cannot give them wives from our daughters," a burly man from the Tribe of Gad spoke up. "For we have sworn an oath, saying, 'Cursed be the one who gives a wife to Benjamin.'"

"Well, there is that," Messiah mused, then settled in with members of his tribe—ones from Naphtali.

"Wait a minute. What about the yearly feast of the Lord in Shiloh?"

Messiah sighed wearily and slapped a hand on his forehead. "Don't you think that—"

"Shut it," an elder snapped.

"No, I won't." Messiah shook a fist toward the man, then focused on scanning the crowd. "Every time you all don't consult with God first, you get *all* of us in trouble. I'm just saying. But you didn't hear that from me." He stepped over a group of men sprawled out near a tree. "When the daughters of Shiloh dance for God, it is a sacred thing. Which means you're going to commit another atrocity, this time against the very God who saved your butts when you all dove in first and thought about things later."

He swept a gaze across the people closest to him. "You went to war with the tribe of Benjamin because they protected men who had raped a woman, and now you want to reward that tribe by snatching these innocent girls while they are performing an act that's sacred to God. That's unthinkable and should not be done. At the risk of sounding redundant, I still have to say it again ... you're going to devastate these girls and their families in order to compensate the very men who protected other men who raped a woman to death!"

Only a few seconds passed before nearly everyone voiced their opinion, which amounted to, "Overruled."

Therefore, they told the men of Benjamin, "Go, lie in wait in the vineyards, and watch. When the daughters of Shiloh come out to perform their dances, rush out from the vineyards. Every man catch a wife for himself from the daughters of Shiloh; then go to the land of Benjamin."

"Oh, that's ripe," Messiah shouted.

The stocky man next to him yanked him down so he wouldn't say anything more.

"But what about the girls' fathers and brothers? Won't they get angry if we do this?" one of the Benjamites asked.

"My point exactly," Messiah said.

"They're going to wrap your mouth with a loin if you don't cut it out," his friend said, trying to keep his voice low.

"Someone has to be the voice of reason," Messiah replied, giving a recap of the series of tragic events that led to thousands of women and children being murdered, and now another scenario where women were going to be taken without proper request or arrangement.

They argued back and forth until the elders conferred and came back with their decision. "When their fathers or their brothers come to us to complain, we'll say, 'Be kind to the Benjamites for our sakes, because we did not leave any wives for them when we fought against them.'"

"The main thing the fathers and brothers of the girls taken from Shiloh will be concerned about is that they are breaking their oath because their daughters are going to be wed to Benjamites. But"—he jutted a wrinkled finger in the air—"they won't be guilty of that because they didn't *give* their daughters to marry Benjamites; the Benjamites *stole* their daughters and married them."

During the ensuing raid, the children of Benjamin took enough wives for their number from those who danced. Then they rebuilt the cities that had been burned to the ground and went back to live in them.

Once that feat was accomplished, the children of Israel departed from there at that time, every man to his tribe and family. They all left happy, every man to his inheritance.

"In those days there was no king in Israel: every man did that which was right in his own eyes." Judges 21:25

Chapter 5

Ask for Direction and Divine Guidance First

My biggest question that has come up in my spiritual walk has been where was God when horrible things happened to me? Why are women less valued than men, or only worthy based on the fact that they can carry a child? Then, in biblical times, and even now—given the recent climate in America.

How was I supposed to believe in a God that would sanction such a thing? And as I went through my spiritual rounds, I couldn't lay this at the foot of one religion, because the value of women and who we are in the world is nearly the same way in all religions that span the globe.

How am I supposed to believe in a God who doesn't seem to believe in me—a woman? This has been a major struggle throughout my spiritual journey. I've been through several religions in my search for truth (what I call the spiritual chit'lin circuit), in my quest to understand why my life began the way it did. Other religions make women second class citizens also, and it has infiltrated politics, the workplace, relationships, and marriages. Except one—the Bahai's Faith—who sees women equally, in all aspects.

In this story, the Levite scattered the concubine's body to twelve tribes, and it started an avalanche of tragedy that affected the women of Gibeah, then the women and children of Jabesh Gilead, and further the daughters of Shiloh. None of them deserved what happened to them. They were all casualties of the faulty thinking of men, who made one mistake after another, mostly without God's counsel.

My life is a great deal like every woman mentioned in this story:

Women who were supposedly forgiven, only to then be tossed to the wolves.
Women who were hurt and harmed through no fault of their own.
Women who were in the wrong place at the wrong time.
Women who were snatched while minding their own business.
Women who were harmed even in the service of God.
Women who were killed because they were connected to the wrong people.

Well, several times throughout this little slice of Biblical history, the Bible states the reason a majority of these atrocious deeds and misdeeds took place was that *"there was no king in the land and every man did what was right in their own eyes."*

So, that assertion was stated for everyone to believe that having a king in place meant that women would be respected and protected. In *Transformation*, another book in this series, I take a look at what happened to King David's daughter,

Tamar. Something that occurred in her story meant those first words—no king in the land—doesn't hold water.

Over the years, I have written several books and some of my main female characters have my personal background as part of their backstory. One particular novel forced me to delve into that central question: Where was God? I was almost ready to go to print, but felt something was missing. Truthfully, I avoided the hard issue of putting the vulnerable parts of myself on the page.

I'm going to share an excerpt from, *Was it Good For You Too?*, my novel that initially addresses this question. It was here this question made its bold appearance, and I was drawn to the answer, one that not only satisfied my soul but poured into the soul of another—a reader ... Maybe her overwhelming need met my vulnerability halfway. I have learned in writing that words have power, and that's why I have to be careful of how characters and situations are portrayed. But in this instance, I answered a reader's question not knowing, in that red-hot moment, that others were waiting for my words to be delivered exactly in the right place and time. What you desire, desires you! What you're looking for is looking for you!

Morning came, and he was still with her, his arms wrapped around her in a safety net she did not feel she deserved.

"If you won't trust me," he whispered, stroking a hand down her back. "Ask God to help you through this."

She stiffened, and a fragment of unease slithered up her spine. "God?" Tailan pulled away to look down on him. "God? Seriously? You want me to ask God for help sorting out my life?" She shook her head. "God forgot about me. Where was God when those men killed my family? Where was God when my uncle raped my mother? Where was God when my uncle raped his children and their children?" She slammed her hand against his chest. "When Amir's sister and father were killed?

When my cousins were killed? Where was God when all of these horrible things happened?" Tears blurred her vision as she asked, "What kind of God would allow people to hurt others this way?"

Delvin closed his eyes against the vehemence in her voice, against the deep-seated anger and pain that he had always felt from her when it came to these matters. He had always skirted around this issue, but today, he realized it spoke to the heart of things when it came to her ability to trust him or anyone, to love him completely or to let him go. He had to meet her where she was.

"I'll tell you where God was," he said in a soft tone as he lifted her chin, so they were eye to eye. "God was whispering in your parents' ears to get you to safety. God was whispering in your mother's ear to give her the strength to tell the world what your uncle had done. God whispered in your ear, urging you to leave the west side that night." His eyes searched her tear-filled ones for a moment. "God whispered in my ear and said I should go into that classroom instead of going home. God whispered in my ear that I should take you home with me and keep you safe—even if I would get in trouble with my parents."

Tears fell from her eyes at a rapid pace.

"God whispered in my ear that I should love you and show you the side of God's love that is spoken of in words and song. God whispered in my mother's ears to make you the daughter she always wanted." On these words, Delvin's voice wavered a little, the emotions coming too fast to keep them at bay. "God whispered in my ear to get my behind on that tour bus and ask your forgiveness for what I did to hurt you. God whispered in Amir's ear and said to make you his wife for that period of time it took for you to heal from the pain I'd caused. God whispered into your womb and planted a child that is the best parts of both of us, and who will bind us for the rest of our lives."

Delvin pulled her head against his chest. "God is right here with us, watching over us, keeping us safe. God is right here in my heart and yours, whether we ever act on that love or we remain apart. God is in the tears that are falling from your eyes, because God knows you need them because you hold in so much."

She was silent for so long, he thought she might have fallen asleep. Then her hand reached up and rested on his cheek.

Delvin kissed her forehead and said, "Those ugly things that you've experienced, that's a man thing, a human thing—the kind that devours, hurts, and harms, the kind that is selfish and evil. That's not of God. God is love. God is everything that is good. The tests and challenges that come from people who don't embrace those parts of God are all about strengthening us, forcing us to draw on The Source, that Higher Power." Delvin held her even tighter. "God put us here to have an abundant life, to live our dreams. We live off the prayers of our ancestors who didn't have nearly as much as we do. But it doesn't mean that we're going to sail through life without some kind of challenges along the way."

Delvin looked down at her. "My challenge right now? To love you, even when you don't feel you deserve that love. To love you in spite of the pain you cause me, every time I'm forced to accept and respect that I am not the leading man in your life." He cupped her face in his hands. "God gives me the strength to get through because it is not easy to love a woman who I feel is rightfully mine and keep enough distance that I'm respecting her marriage vows. I ask God for strength every single day because I need it now more than I ever did." He locked a gaze with her. "That's the kind of God I believe in, Tai … and in time, I hope you will too. Then you'll stop searching elsewhere for the very thing that you already have."

Delvin gathered her into his arms, holding her while she cried out for her loss, for her pain, her anger at the being that created them and every living thing on earth.

"It's all right to be angry at God, Tai," Delvin said in a breathy whisper. "God can take it. God's a pretty big God. Can handle anything. You'll see."

Her smile was fleeting, but it was there. And it was a sure sign that Delvin was reaching her on some level.

Honestly, I cry every time when reading that part of the book because it speaks to my soul. Everyone has a path, and evidently mine traveled a route that had tragic origins and even more tragic outcomes. The reader I spoke of earlier sent me a message letting me know that being vulnerable was the thing that was needed to help her . . .

Faysha: Just finished *Was it Good for You Too*! I loved the book, but more than anything, I walked away feeling renewed. I was struggling with my faith because of all of the terrible stuff going on in the world (especially with children). I was borderline ready to start taking Religion courses in an effort to deepen my understanding. As the novel ended, my question was answered exactly like I needed to hear it. EXACTLY. Thank you so much for this novel—it was just what I needed at this point in my life.

Naleighna Kai: Faysha, that is soooo powerful. You must be talking about that Where was God? scene. Brought me to tears every single time!!

Faysha: Yassss! I had a mini praise break after that part. My circle of people are very spiritual, and I didn't have one person that could answer my question in a way that could comfort me and make me understand. This did it. Call me crazy but I honestly think God needed me to read that part in 100% silence/peace. I've tried reading bits and pieces because the "read while the kids nap" plan didn't work. I got right up to that part and couldn't read until it was truly peaceful. It's because it is what I needed. I seriously can go to sleep peacefully.

Naleighna Kai: You have blessed me tonight. Thank you so much for sharing this. Authors need to know that our work is not just about entertainment, but we truly share a message that can touch the soul. I know that scene was something that spoke to me. I've been afraid to ask that question out loud after all these years and the horrible things that happened. But the answer that came from within as I wrote the book, and having it come from a man that truly now understood what unconditional love was all about—made it more dynamic in my eyes. Sometimes, I write to heal ... *Me!!!*

Chapter 6

What's the lesson in all of this?

Once I came across a statement that said, a person might have been through years of traumatic experiences or abuse, but it doesn't have to take that same amount of years for them to heal.

Where was God when all of these things happened? What things?, you ask.

What had happened was . . . I was adopted by my biological mother. Yes, you read that right. On the day I was born, my mother signed herself into the hospital as her sister, Rose. Then, she pushed until I emerged from her body, dropped me into my aunt's arms, left the hospital, and didn't look back. Until fate gave her no other choice.

My "new" mother/aunt raised me for eighteen months, then made a disastrous mistake that earned her a trip to prison.

What a family, right?

Unfortunately, I landed back in the one place my biological mother never wanted me to be—her home. To make matters worse, after swallowing some type of household cleaner, I ended up with a medical emergency which put me in the hospital for weeks. My biological mother was forced to go before the judge and tell the truth about what she'd done when I was first born. The result? I was adopted by my biological mother.

Here is where things in my life became more interesting. When I first arrived at that three-bedroom apartment in the Robert Taylor Homes, a project on the South Side of Chicago, I went directly to my mother's friend—whom I had never laid eyes on before—crawled into her lap, and went to sleep. That woman became someone I call my "true mother".

My biological mother had been through a great deal, and later on, the manner of my conception came to light—from what I understand, my father forced my mother—this added insult to life's already plentiful set of injuries. She was bitter and angry at having to raise the very child she wanted nothing to do with—for obvious reasons. She had taken every precaution to ensure there were no reminders, but was thwarted. All the measures she took to abort me—pills, hangers, and physically abusing herself—had failed.

Evidently, there were some life lessons for us to learn from that entire scenario, because the physical and emotional abuse I endured was substantial. The only person who tried to protect me was my true mother, who stayed in an emotionally abusive friendship far longer than was practical. All because she felt the need to be there for me.

Once, she did try to leave, but was immediately compelled to return because I had endured an even more horrific ordeal. At age fourteen, I was curvaceous and built like the proverbial brick house—which attracted the wrong kind of male attention.

Transition: From Forgotten to Forgiven and Highly Favored

Adult male attention.

I had run away to live with Aunt Rose—that "first" mother for the initial eighteen months of my life. She had served her prison sentence and was back in Chicago.

After overhearing a conversation where Aunt Rose was making arrangements for her brother—my uncle—to visit her house every week to have sex with me, I realized my safety was not a given, even around her. Trust me, I didn't stick around to find out the end result of that trade. Instead, I fled to the supposed safety of my father's home.

My mother had kept the secret of what my father had done to her, so I didn't realize living with him wouldn't make me any safer than being with her or my aunt. Because this book is about not only trials but also triumphs, I'll state this simply: my father didn't respect my right to say no, and I endured two months of pure hell. This was compounded by the fact that the ordeal happened during the summer, when no school officials or teachers would come looking for me because there was no place I was "supposed" to be. No one knew I was "missing". No one knew I had run to him.

He made the mistake of untying me from the portable cot that was my existence for several weeks at a time. While he was escorting me on an infrequent trip to the bathroom, somehow I had enough strength left to bolt for the window, prepared to die so I could finally put an end to that nightmare.

Breaking through the glass, instead of crashing into a crumpled, bloody mess on the concrete, I actually landed on my feet. The shock of that effort ripped through me. As traffic passed by on Michigan Avenue, I stood there, amazed at coming through in one piece. No broken bones, only small cuts from the glass. Totally naked. Starved and undernourished, much thinner than when I arrived two months prior, and probably looking a frightful mess. Which would make sense given what had transpired.

Two women who were having a smoke on the porch quickly gathered me up. They ushered me inside their apartment before my father could put his clothes on and make it down the stairs. They were about to call the police, but I stopped them. My father carried two holstered guns and some type of badge. I wasn't sure what type of agency he worked for, but knew he was great friends with several police officers in that area. Police would not be of any help. So I asked the women to call the one person who I never thought would be in my life again.

My biological mother.

On the way home, while sitting in the back of my brother's navy-blue Chevy Caprice, wearing clothes that the women had given me after they bathed me, she tried to get me to talk about what happened. I didn't talk. I didn't cry. I was numb, tired, and still afraid that even she wouldn't protect me. Besides, she had already done enough damage to me on her own.

Then my mother twisted the knife my father's abuse had anchored in my back. "Whatever happened to you was good for you."

Yes, she actually said that without knowing what he'd done. Only later when writing the novel, *She Touched My Soul*, did I understand that she probably *did* know, because he'd done the same thing to her. But with just those few words, her need to always be right and to punish me for embarrassing her by running away, returned me to the natural order of things. Yes, I was home. Back to the norm of emotional assault, and abuse that I could actually welcome after being held hostage in one of my father's many apartments for two months.

Thankfully, my true mother returned the moment she found out I was back at the house on Merrion Avenue. She was the one who helped me at the beginning stages of healing.

Unfortunately, it would be years before the real healing took place.

Chapter 7

Unexpected Occurrences

The first and biggest challenge has been releasing those parts of me, at my core, that kept me feeling unsafe. The second, was how I would raise a male child without infecting him with all the pain from my past.

At age seventeen, I dated a twenty-five-year-old man named Al. And three months later after I turned eighteen, wouldn't you know it? I found myself with child in no time flat.

Now from Al's point of view, it was my intention to get pregnant. In his mind, he had every right to be angry. With me, he thought he was getting a mature woman (at seventeen?) who had handled her business, which meant he could have all the fun and none of the side effects. Good luck with that. Especially since he didn't consistently use protection. And truth be told, though I didn't want to get pregnant, I didn't consistently do what it took *not* to get pregnant.

So there I was about two months along, and he had to tell his mother. She had some not-so-nice things to say about the situation. Even though she spoke her disdain of me in her native language, I could still understand the N-word, the B-word, and the W-word or its derivatives.

I asked him, "Are you going to let her talk about me that way?"

To which he replied, "What do you expect me to say? That's my mother."

"Looks like you'll be sleeping with your mama from this point on," I shot back.

For the record, I wasn't Little Miss Sunshine, so I didn't say "sleeping", but I'm trying to keep this book rated P.G.

When I first found out I was pregnant, my true mother had left the house on Merrion again after a particularly horrible argument with my biological mother. So I ran away to stay with my uncle and his wife. That was when another family member molested me, for the second time.

By the end of my pregnancy, I was nearly twice the size I had been before. When I weaned my son after breastfeeding, I was off the charts at over two hundred-fifty pounds. The added bulk I carried was the hiding place for my pain, my sorrow, my guilt, my "what ifs", my anger, my rage, my "victimhood", and my lost childhood. They regularly invited the Lack family—lack of discipline, lack of self-worth, and lack of self-love—to shack up with them in the abyss that was my soul. And as inconsiderate houseguests sometimes do, they flung the door open so everything else that weighed me down could cram in beside them. There was no more room, but all the things that tried to destroy so much in me, all the experiences that took away my ability to trust, to love, to hope, to have joy, and to have peace, pushed their way inside just the same.

The wheel of child support fortune didn't end until I let my son's father go, forgave him, and forgave myself. The last was the hardest. All those years, I had been resentful of the fact that *he* got me pregnant and then quickly abandoned me and continuously abandoned his son. He hurt my son on a number of occasions with false promises of spending time with him, then failing to show—because it was the only way to hurt me. He was resentful that not only did I get pregnant and alter his life, but the child that came out of that union was a reminder that he would forever pay for one of those many nights when we were closer than close.

Same situation, different views. All anger, frustration, resentment, and pain.

So let's take a look at things. I was seventeen and in college at the time, and he was twenty-five. We were from two different cultures and backgrounds, and our approach to life was very different. We started dating when I *mysteriously* became pregnant a few months later at age eighteen, that in order to avoid child support, he became a professional student, which meant he never did anything substantial with the four degrees he earned. Al still had to pay that child support anyway.

Let's move on to my son. At age fifteen, a frightening response to an English assignment led to him writing a book and being published at age sixteen. The assignment was to write a scary story. While other students wrote horror film type of work, my son wrote what it would be like if he was forced to kill one parent to protect another. Yes, that's some scary stuff right there. They called me up to the school to speak with several officials, only to find out that a great deal of it was pure fiction. I paired him up with a developmental editor, and he took one year to write the book in between his studies.

While on a college tour, he gave a copy to an admission's director and eventually landed a presidential scholarship to Fisk University. He then acquired a book deal with Simon & Schuster for his second novel and a nomination for an NAACP Image Award for Outstanding Literature. He took me with him to the red carpet. This is just the tip of his personal accomplishments, all achieved before the age of twenty-one. Eventually, he shifted gears and now does book cover tutorials for one of the leading graphic software companies and brand management for top-tier clients, along with traveling the world.

His father is now sixty-two years old, never moved out of his mother's home, and is still working a job where he's just ambling toward retirement. Meanwhile, that seventeen-year-old girl he impregnated, has owned two homes (the first one purchased at age nineteen), is now a *USA TODAY* Bestselling author, a literary agent, a book coach, and a book whisperer who helps others tell their stories.

I always feared infecting my son with the aftermath of my tragic past, with the damage inflicted by my mother, father, and uncle. But upon hearing what his fiancée recently said about him during a surprise proposal, "You are things I didn't think to ask God for," I realized the difference between my son and his father. While raising him, I never gave my son the idea that he couldn't do anything he set his mind to. I didn't let him buy into the lack and limitation, or poverty mindset that I had been born into. So, he's destined to be greater than even I aspired to be. And I've learned a great deal from his journey; he's teaching me so much about valuing myself and what I bring to the world.

Releasing one's deep-seated issues helps the emotional, mental, and financial parts of life fall in line. The year I took my son's advice, forgave his father, and released the child-support battle, was the same year something miraculous happened in my literary life.

The more successful self-published authors became in matching the sales of traditional publishing houses, the tighter the publisher's controls became. They made it harder for self-published authors to get into bookstores. We could no longer directly talk to managers at Borders and Waldenbooks to do signings. Now we had to work with a distributor and were sent through hoops to land on the shelves. The process was challenging, and I finally wanted a book deal with a major house.

I went to Book Expo America, a publishing industry convention where agents, editors, and movie producers were all in one place for a three day period. I gave away fifty copies of my book, *Every Woman Needs a Wife*. One of those copies landed in the hands of an acquisition editor for Simon & Schuster. Two weeks later, while attending a Tee C. Royal event in Atlanta, I received a call advising that I had a fax at the front desk. When I retrieved it, it was a contract for me—and a separate contract for my teenage son—to sign with Simon & Schuster. The acquisition editor tracked us down to give us that deal with no prior negotiation.

My aim was to attract a way to be published without the restrictions placed on self-publishing. I didn't focus on the how; I focused on that one intention. I purposefully went with the desire to be with a major house, and out of the thousands of authors who attended, I attracted the very thing I desired.

The same year, I hit that national bestsellers list for the first time. Also, I received a royalty check that was more than the amount of back child support my son's father paid in seven years. During that time, my son received a royalty check from Simon & Schuster that covered his school expenses. Then, he was nominated for an NAACP image award.

Have things been unfair in your life and seemingly not in your favor? Probably. It's up to you—and only you—to change that. Who do you need to forgive? What do you need to let go? The Creator has more in store for you, but you have to release and recover from the things that have tried to take you out of the game before it even started.

Chapter 8

Breaking Generational Curses

Most of the females in my immediate family have not escaped their share of traumatic experiences.

A thirty-five-year-old man raped my sister, Eve, in church when she was eight. That set her on a destructive path that led her to run away from home at age seventeen with an ex-con who worked in the lunchroom at her high school. This was long before they did background checks on people working in schools.

She would spend years selling herself on the streets, working to get the next high that her pimp provided to keep her making money for him. From what I understand, she miscarried about nine children during those years due to the physical abuse she suffered.

Eve returned home when I was ten or eleven, scalded from her neck to lower back. A going away present from a pimp who was none too happy because she tried to leave. She had no choice but to wear a halter-top on the bus ride from Memphis to Chicago. She sat with her face leaning against the seatback in front of her because the third-degree burns had melted away the top two layers of skin, leaving the pink flesh underneath exposed.

My biological mother and my true mother spent an eternity in Cook County Hospital waiting for Eve to receive treatment. They patched her up, gave her some meds, and she was on the first thing smoking back to Memphis—and him.

Years later, she returned home to Chicago again. Eve was nothing like the smart, beautiful girl she'd been before. Time on the streets had put twenty extra years on her, made her greedy, self-serving, and willing to hurt the ones she was supposed to love if it meant getting what she wanted. She tried to flow into a regular life, but the change in her was so profound she would never be "normal" again.

Eventually she became pregnant with my beautiful niece, LaKecia, but was unable to care for her or the son that came a few years after. The Department of Children and Family Services took both of them, due to neglect, and placed them with my biological mother and true mother. My niece, who we believe had been molested by one of my sister's boyfriends at age five, ran away from home and my mother's strict rules at age fourteen, following in her mother's unfortunate footsteps. Only LaKecia's pimp wasn't a stranger. He was the son of one of my mother's church friends. Once or twice, the police picked my niece up, and she had more than a grand in her pockets from a single night's work.

LaKecia came to live with me when she turned nineteen. By that time, she'd been diagnosed as a manic-depressive and paranoid schizophrenic, possibly triggered by genetics and whatever drugs her pimp was giving her to keep her working. Though I didn't totally understand the conditions, I did learn enough to help her improve and start going back to school, and then to church. She expressed her dreams and goals and made plans to be successful. And when she laughed or was excited about achieving some of the things she planned, the world seemed all right. Hanging with my son helped her a great deal, which is funny because she'd bitten his foot when he was a newborn because she thought he was a doll.

The social worker said LaKecia had never looked so beautiful, or seemed so happy before. We only had issues when she tried to skip taking her meds, which is common for that illness. Otherwise, my niece was on the path to becoming whatever she desired.

Then my sister happened.

Though boundaries were in place to protect my niece from herself, I didn't realize she needed to be protected from her mother. Three rules existed in my house—finish school, no dating for a while, and be home at a reasonable hour. In hindsight, maybe restrictions should have been in place regarding contact with her mother.

Eve, who still hadn't healed from her own experiences, promised LaKecia the world to coerce her to leave my house and come to hers. Eventually my niece fell for those promises, believing that being able to do everything she wanted and no longer having to live within my boundaries was a better life. She moved back into the childhood home that my sister had "taken over" when my mother made her transition.

This was a match made in hell.

The house was shot into several times one night because my sister owed money to people who weren't interested in waiting for the first or third of the month to get their dollars. Soon, the dealers took over the house and everything—*and everyone*—in it. Including my niece. They owned her, too, forcing her to work off a debt that wasn't hers to begin with.

Unfortunately, LaKecia was now back in a position that was the polar opposite of the achievements she'd made in recent months. And nothing could be done. Several times, I offered to get her out of the house. Even brought the police with me once to make sure that the answers she gave me were of her own accord. Because she was an adult, no one could force her to leave, not even the officers.

That was the beginning of things going from bad to worse.

Now she was in a hell of her own making due to choices that were not in her best interest. Despite not having the bandwidth to fight a battle she obviously didn't want me to win, I still wanted my niece to be all right.

All told, she barely survived living in that house and was in and out of mental facilities for a few years. Finally, my true mother had her placed in a facility called Hargrove. LaKecia came home on the weekends, and she stayed with me occasionally. She was improving. In the back of my mind, there would be enough time for me to save up the kind of money that would get her the right meds—shots instead of the pills she sometimes refused to take—along with counseling with Sesvalah, the woman who gave me the tools I needed to heal from my abuse.

That vision never materialized, but not through any fault of her own. LaKecia went into an office at Hargrove one day and told one of the high-ranking employees that she wanted to go back to school. He said, "Why? You'll *never* have more than a fourteen-year-old mentality."

My niece's spirit and energy took a nosedive. While her body had been through some traumatic experiences, my firm belief is that his statement had dealt her so much of an emotional, spiritual, and mental blow, she was ready to leave this earth.

I was well aware of the mental and developmental issues that resulted from the drugs that had devastated her body, but I would never, ever kill the dream of someone who wanted to try. And the worst part is that he was just flat-out wrong! LaKecia had finished some schooling at a higher level while she was living with me, so I know he was way off base.

She died two weeks later. Life and death are in the power of the tongue.

Trying is growth. Growth is evolving. Evolving is the very thing that we, spiritual beings with a human experience, are supposed to do. In my heart of hearts, I believe LaKecia's desire to strive for excellence would have made all the difference in her life. She would rather have tried and failed, than to be told that she'd never, *ever* achieve anything worthwhile.

I know the power of The Creator and how wonderful life can be when The Creator puts the right people in your path at the right time. It is how I exist today—believing that anything and everything is possible. Including overcoming the limitations that others try to put on my life. I'm constantly striving to rise above the past situations—abuse, molestation, and torture—that pointed me in the opposite direction of The Creator's intended destination for me, long before I even attempted to get out of the gate.

Sometimes I equate what happened to me at the beginning of my life to a game of Spades. In a game of Spades, the hand you're dealt can be so bad that you go in the "hole"—in the negative on a point scale—not knowing if you'll be able to get out again. Then it takes bidding a "blind six" or a "blind seven" just to get back on the board. Just to get back to zero. That blind bid takes place before the cards are even dealt, and it's a risk because either the player makes it and they're back in the game, or they don't and they're even further in the negative.

My niece once took a photo during a shoot for the cover of my novel, My Time in the Sun. The picture had a lilac background and she stood in the foreground draped in a royal purple and gold scarf. The make-up artist had applied hues of lavender to complement her golden skin. She was a princess, and more beautiful than ever. My niece's hand was cupped in a pose where the graphic designer would place an image of her own personal sun. No one could look at that image and detect the hell she had been through. This is an image of her that I hold in my heart to this day.

That photo of LaKecia Janise Woodson is also a reminder that whenever anyone comes to me wanting to do something to reach their dreams or get on a healing path, I will try, to the best of my ability, to help them get back in the game.

When first working on this text while at the Essence Music Festival in New Orleans for a book signing, I was by the pool, stretched out on the lounger. I fell asleep and dreamed of LaKecia for the first time in ages. Her image first came through as a baby in my arms. Then a few minutes later, she was a toddler, smiling and laughing and holding on to me. In the dream, tears streamed down my face because I was so happy to see her.

Upon awakening, the ugly reality greeted me. I still felt guilty and had so many regrets. *If only* I had cut my book tour short and used that money to move her back in with me instead of letting my true mother put her in Hargrove. *If only* I had worked harder at forcing the police to make her come home with me that day. *If only* I had loosened those boundaries, then she would have stayed with me instead of going to her mother. In my mind, men had used and abused her, and I thought she needed to give her body a break. The restrictions I imposed were intended to protect and help her to heal.

If only ... then, maybe then, she would still be here on the earth scene.

The dream came to me for several reasons. She wanted me

to know she was all right, and I needed to release the guilt and regret. Guilt and regret are just as powerful as fear, worry, and doubt. Releasing these emotions has been one of the biggest challenges for me. At one point, I said to The Creator, you took my mother, my brother, and my niece, and left my trifling sister on this earth? What reason could you have for that?

Chapter 9

Jennifer: The Lady of Jeffrey Manor

Everyone has lessons and a path. Sometimes, though, it is painful to see the ones we love go through the challenges. Sometimes we don't get a "do over" with that person, but we get a chance to forge a "do better" with someone else.

For example, Jennifer, who is another niece of mine, reconnected with my son and me when she became an adult. She follows a lot of my Facebook posts and one about "Add on fathers" sparked a dialogue between us where she was able to get an understanding of who her father—my brother—actually was. The conversation filled a lot of the "gaps" and "silences" in her mind. I didn't make excuses for him, just gave her my understanding of the truth.

A couple of months after she had her baby girl, she told me some horrific experiences she had during those years when we'd lost touch. She expressed regret about that period, considering it and other ill-advised decisions a waste of time.

My reply was that she shouldn't regret that time or those experiences because she was stronger than she gave herself credit for. Through her own traumas, she learned what she didn't want in her life, and it propelled her towards the things that she did desire.

Jennifer is now a wife to a man who waited a long time to be with her. She's the mother of their three beautiful children and is excelling in her career in the medical profession. What I love about my niece is that she embraces life and has balance. She has a man in her life who loves her unconditionally—makes her happy. That's a bonus. That's what I want for her most of all.

Once I also posted on Facebook about an interesting incident where three pre-teens were with me for a visit. Anyone who knows me understands that I'm not a "children" person to begin with, so regaling everyone with some things my goddaughters did during that weekend brought some hilarious responses. When one of them landed in trouble, I posted, *I don't spank other people's children. J.L. (my son), don't give me the side-eye.* My niece responded on that post with *Well, here's my side-eye.* I couldn't help laughing. She and her brother were wonderful children, and I enjoyed having them over for visits. Only had to have a "come to Jesus meeting" with them one time, and they were straight from that point on.

She recalls that, but what she mostly remembers is the "cool" aunt who took them to Six Flags Great America for three days in a row. I booked hotel rooms for the weekend and invited an even amount of boys and girls. For three whole days, they were able to visit the amusement park from the time it opened until it closed. The "cool" aunt was chilling in the hotel right across the street. They were old enough and knew the drill on watching out for each other. That's how I did things back then, and it was much safer than now. She reminisces about that with so much love.

One of my finest moments with Jennifer was when she told me how much my words have helped her. And a memory of when she first entered the womanhood stage of life and I came over and took her shopping. Her mother allowed me to be the one to have that special moment. My niece has forever held that experience close to her heart.

One of the greatest purposes I have in life is to help others or to inspire them to achieve a level they never thought possible. So having the conversation with her about "regrets" provided her with insight from my own experiences. What's in the past cannot be changed. We can only learn and grow from it. We can't go back and rewrite it or take back hurtful words or actions. We can do what we can to right old wrongs, but if the other person is not receptive—move on. Don't let others hold guilt over you and make you "pay" for something the rest of your life.

Writing is now a family affair. A few days before 2020 came in, I made a decision (or the decision was made for me by The Creator) that I would give back to my family first. I have spared a lot of time and energy to everyone else for twenty years, but believed my family should be heard. The family scribes: My son, J. L. Woodson (who hadn't written anything since his NAACP Image Award nomination as a teen); my niece J. S. Cole, who had never written before; and my nephew, Hiram Shogun Harris, who some of you might have seen on *Black Ink Chicago/9 Mag* as a tattoo artist. Hiram didn't balk but only asked for some peach cobbler when he came over to write his book.

My niece and I penned a book last year, *Lady of Jeffrey Manor*, and it shares some issues that she had not told another living soul. Abandonment. Parts of her that were missing sounded so familiar. Her issues stemmed from boyfriends—physical, verbal, and mental abuse.

Jennifer had never aspired to write a book. I called her three days after Christmas and told her she was writing one for the "Knights of the Castle" series because it was time for me to give back to family, the way I had given to everyone else.

She had never taken a class, but had read my book on writing. Here's how her book progressed from start to finish. She typed the majority of it on her iPhone—texted or emailed it to me. Midway through the process, I feared she would compromise her fingers and hand and it could affect her job. She's a surgical tech nurse and all that typing on the phone was going to have long-lasting results. I gave her my computer, and she kept at it. She went through the rewriting phase, then members of NK's Tribe Called Success kicked into gear to help bring the novel to the finish line. National Bestselling Author, J. L. Campbell—editor for content, Stephanie M. Freeman—editor for flow, U. M. Hiram for fleshing out a few concepts, Ellen Kiley Goeckler—Beta, Debra J. Mitchell—Beta, Brynn Weimer—Beta, Kelsie Maxwell—Beta.

After each person touched the work, she had to go in and do more rewrites. I'm so proud she didn't doubt her ability. Instead, she just kept asking, "All right, so what's next?"

When I brought her an advanced copy of the book to hold, it took a few moments for her to get over the shock and happiness. Then she cried. The work, the amount of time, my paying double for the advance to make it prior to release—was all worth it. Now this is someone who didn't aspire to write—just like me—and she actually did the doggone thing. Do not doubt that you are able to do the same.

My niece went to work one day and saw staff-wide congratulations for her book on the bulletin board. Someone had learned about her book from social media, and everyone came by to wish her well. I'm so happy for my niece. Family support. Work support. Tribe support. Not everyone has this experience.

I don't know what it is, but you can hold a side hustle all day long, but something about telling someone you wrote a book can make people feel some kind of way. "I've always wanted to write a book ..." or "So can you write my life story?" or "People always said my life should be a book ..." When my niece sent a photo of the congratulatory board from her job, my heart swelled with pride. Yes, we can give 150% to our day jobs and still give 150% to ourselves.

In my entire publishing life, the experience of writing with family members and the Tribe has been my most successful venture. Not only did my son, niece, and nephew bring new voices to the book series they wrote in, they also brought in a new audience, people who hadn't heard of me or my Tribe. How do I know they've been doing well? Two of the releases—*Lady of Jeffrey Manor* and *Knight of Grand Crossing*—did even better than my own release in the series. I am so proud of that. My son's book, *Knight of Irondale*, was well received because people have been waiting for something from him for years. And the entire process brought us closer because they were able to share things with me that we hadn't discussed before. The written word is powerful, and adding my family to the Tribe has been an amazing thing.

My niece is now working on her next book, and my nephew already had thoughts of a memoir based on his own tragic experience. My son, well, he might write a little something, but his heart is set on the graphic/cover design end of things. He has designed for my clients and the series for the last five years. As Ice Cube said, "Today is a good day." And I'll add, there are a few more pens that now "slay". Yes, it rhymes. Don't give me that side-eye.

And yes, my nephew walked off with a whole pan of peach cobbler. To be honest, I'm not sure if he shared it with anyone.

Chapter 10

My True Mother

After a little background work and a few phone calls that went up the chain, I was able to see my true mother in the nursing home where she now lives. For the first time in a year, they allowed me to have a compassionate care visit with her. My aim was to tell my mother that I love and forgive her.

She made the decision to be in a relationship with someone who forced her to choose between me or her. What I know about my true mother is that she consistently finds herself in situations where she loves the partner more than the partner loves her. First, with my biological mother, who resented their connection. Two years into their relationship, my biological mother embraced religion and made everyone's life a living hell because she had to deny her true inclination—being attracted to women.

Then yet another woman came into her life and this one was emotionally unavailable to my true mother. This final woman was embroiled in a restrictive religion and also resented my true mother. At the beginning of that relationship, my true mother almost emptied my accounts wining and dining on my dime. I paid off credit cards, and the balances crept back up. When I researched what was going on, it hurt my heart. My true mother had given the appearance that she had a lot more money than she actually did in reality.

The woman fell for her, thinking she was rich. I cut off every one of those cards, and the romancing dried up. They were having a good run. A *very* good run. But I had to tighten ship, since having my finances together was important to me. My mother's lover gave me the cold shoulder for a long time after that.

Now for the hard part. This new woman was as emotionally abusive as my biological mother had been—maybe even more, because my true mother was older and certainly more vulnerable. I had to wonder, why did she keep attracting this same scenario into her life? First my biological mom, who became angry, bitter, and unfulfilled when she ended the intimate parts of their relationship the moment religion and judgment dropped in for a visit and stayed far past their welcome.

Now, the woman was bitter at the fact that I put the brakes on my finances that funded their romance. So bitter that when they moved in together, she put restrictions on my true mother seeing me. I felt abandoned and hurt all over again.

For the first time in almost thirty years, she was in love again. Love can make you do foolish things. But you can't do foolish things that can alter the path of someone else's life. Especially the life of someone with a goal that will benefit the entire family.

Several other things happened during that time. My best

friend, who had moved to Chicago to escape an abusive husband who nearly made good on a promise to kill her, purposely deleted an email to me from a woman who was Stephen King's agent at the time. The agent was asking to take a look at both of the books I had written. I only found out what happened because my son installed some type of software on the computer and it accidentally restored all the deleted emails and made them visible again in the inbox. When confronted, my friend admitted she was afraid that if I became too successful, then she would somehow lose me as a friend.

She did lose me. Trust and loyalty are very important to me.

My biological mother died during that time, and she left money to my siblings—which wasn't a bad thing. But she left the *responsibility* of her final arrangements to my brother. We almost didn't get her buried because he was listening to my sister (yes, *that* sister. They have the same mother and father, but we only share the same mother). They both believed that the insurance and pension money was for them and expected me to pay for the funeral out of my pocket. Mind you, there was more than enough insurance to cover everything for her final resting.

Days before the funeral, I stopped answering their calls. My sister's husband started stalking my home in Burnham, a suburb of Chicago. Definitely several miles from where they lived. That's when I realized that I needed a change in my life and location. I wrote about all of this in *The Pleasure's All Mine*.

I packed what I could carry for myself and my son and left the house I had purchased for me, my son, my true mother, and my nephew, Eric, to live in. I turned everything over to the people under my roof—my mother, her grandson, her new lover, and my friend who had tried to derail my literary career. They could all work it out on their own.

For an entire year, I lived in the heart of an impoverished neighborhood. Sometimes, my son and I would sleep on the floor to avoid the nightly gunshots. Finally, one night I said, "No more. We're sleeping in our beds. If there's a bullet with our names on it, it'll meet us wherever we are."

My son moved me out of that place before he went off to Fisk University because he didn't want to worry about me. That was one of the best things he could have ever done.

Later, illness set in for my true mother. Even bigger problems ensued that involved me bringing the authorities over to make them aware of how she was being neglected, and to have her placed in the hospital for emergency care. This was followed by placement into rehab and long-term care. I firmly believe that even though this created more dissension, it was the right thing to do. She had so many untreated health issues that she could have died.

Life happened and the partner ended up in a facility herself. This opened the way for me to have unrestricted access to my true mother. On that first visit, she said my name for the first time in seven years. Said my name! She sometimes mistakes me for her sister, but if I'm sitting with her long enough, she'll remember my name. She had not before that time.

The last time I saw her, shortly after pandemic-related restrictions on visits to the nursing home were lifted, she not only remembered my name, she sang it. I recorded it to keep it close to my heart. I was able to tell her that I love and forgive her. She said, "I love you, and there's nothing you've ever done to me that needs my forgiveness."

Chapter 11

To forgive or Not to Forgive

At one time, while writing a novel titled *She Touched My Soul* and giving the character a little of my background in her experience with her mother, I told The Creator that if the reason she hated me so much was that a certain set of things happened to her, then I would be able to forgive her.

When I let my true mother read the manuscript, she said, "Who told you?"

What? No one had told me anything. It was all fiction, right? Unknown to me at the time, some scenes I created in the novel actually happened in real life. So I had no choice but to keep my word, and work on doing what it took to forgive my mother.

Fate is usually seen as something set in stone, something that predetermines the course of events in our lives—or we say that things are meant to be. The basic blueprint of our lives was planned—or predestined—before we were born, to give us the right opportunities for spiritual growth. But we don't have to follow the predestined route and that is why being on the earth scene, being grouped here with all of these interesting souls on a spiritual journey of their own, provides such blessings and lessons.

And this is also where the law of attraction comes in. Think of our life plan like a puzzle, and that our life's purpose is to complete that puzzle. We don't know where all the pieces fit right out of the gate. But as life goes on, we see that people, experiences, our thoughts and actions factor into us evolving; it also adds to spiritual growth.

Fate is sometimes seen as negative or even Karma. When someone does something to us, the first thought is that Karma will take care of it. Do we think that way when someone does something amazing to us? Not necessarily, but we should.

Let's look at families. It's said you don't get to choose your family members. Yet, they give you your first life lessons, and most times they're the reasons you need therapy and spiritual growth. But you can choose your soul families, the people who can help you heal from the experiences you've had in life—including the not so positive ones imprinted on you by your biological family.

My Healing Circle:

See, I didn't have a choice with my family. They were the springboard of pain and life lessons that colored my view of the world and caused a need for healing.

So for my friends, I choose them, cultivate them—and most of them came because of my healing process. My writing allowed me to put my pain on the page. The page became my passion, and the passion became my purpose. Friendship is defined by our collective experiences together.

There is a saying that a woman needs:
a man who cooks
a man who cleans
a man who pays the bills
a man who makes toe-curling, mind-altering love.
And none of these four men should ever be in her house at the same time.

Honestly, I think it's the same for our sister circle of friends. You'll have your apples, your oranges, your grapes, and your cherries, different qualities, different purposes, each serving a different aspect in life, some of them lasting longer than others. Some have to go into the fridge in order to give them a longer shelf life. For others, a man can come between them and their sister circle of friends because they are intimidated by the relationship. Certain connections in our sister circle will go bad no matter what we do. When we don't recognize this, we end up staying in a friendship long past its expiration date, allowing it to stink up the joint. The same way it happens in intimate relationships and families.

My writing also changed the people who were around me. And my life, my inner circle, is filled with people who love me unconditionally. In this book, I'll focus on the women, but in Transformation, Book 9 of this series, I focus on the men.

Rev. Renee Sesvalah Cobb-Dishman

This woman right here had a great part in leading me to my purpose, healing, and overcoming pain-obstacles-challenges. I didn't know writing a novel could help with that.

Sesvalah encouraged me to continue writing as my form of therapy. Six novels came through within a two-year period. Publishing books helped me work through my issues by using fictional characters. This journey has been nothing short of amazing and powerful.

Eventually, I "encouraged" Sesvalah to write a book of her own, *Speak it into Existence*. I'm still waiting for book two—*As Clear as a Bell*—but that first one was a major win.

So, with all the traumatic and painful things that have happened, it took some time before I found a way to forgive, heal, and share my truth at every opportunity.

When I needed to learn love, my son was dropped into my womb.

When I finally needed to heal, Sesvalah, my sexual abuse counselor, entered my life.

When I needed to learn compassion and understanding, my friends Debra and Janice walked in.

When I needed to learn about a God that was unlike the one I knew growing up, Sesvalah, Janine, Janice, Pastor Karen, and Louise Hay became the people who gave the kind of guidance that made a lasting impact.

My experiences speak to the fact that we all carry a vibration that will only attract people who are like us at our innermost core—or the person we are evolving into. That same vibration will carry into all aspects of life—but it requires recognizing it, applying it, and affirming it on a daily basis.

Have you been speaking "life" into your personal, spiritual, financial, and physical circumstances? What are you doing to reclaim your position, your victory over the seemingly negative situations you face? Every day that you open your eyes, take a solid breath, and realize that The Creator has allowed one more day on the journey for you to manifest the very things that you desire. That includes healing.

Debra J.

Debra is the sister-friend who has been with me since the beginning of my writing career. She worked with my mother and was the first to buy my debut novel when I had a book signing in downtown Chicago. She owns every copy and edition of all the books I've written and released, and even those I didn't release. Not only has she continually been one of the absolute biggest supporters of my work, she helped me tone down some darker elements in my books. The sad and painful backstories of characters that mirrored my life too closely were not something Debra liked to read. Nonetheless, she read them because she was aware of the things that happened to me. I have since learned to realize the impact they may have on the reader, and not include such sordid details. I'm thankful she finally said something because for a long time she had stayed silent on that front, knowing I had to tell my truth.

Janice M. Allen

Janice taught me the value of being a good sister-friend. She started as a co-worker who read one of my books, came back and pointed out a few errors, and became one of my editors from that day forward. Later she became a fellow author because I pushed her (kicking and screaming) into writing a novel. She has now published four of them, so the journey must have been good to her. One of the greatest parts of our friendship is that she, along with others close to me, tells me when I'm not quite right about things. That's how friends grow. Not from simply having a cheerleading team, but a cheering-on team. And once, I had to cheer her on from the sidelines.

See, I'm that friend who will love you where you are. Janice taught me to be that nonjudgmental sister-friend who might see you in a bad marriage, but be able to say, "When you're ready to leave, I got you. If you're staying in, I got you." Sometimes, we push our friends and family to live up to our expectations when they're not ready. This might cause them to break away from a bad situation, but they won't stay gone because they followed *your* heart, while *their own* heart and mind were not ready to create a new life without that person by their side.

And you also need to have discernment, as well. On the day in the fall of 2014 when my friend's marriage imploded, she was in the car with me. I was afraid the agreeable, peaceful, docile Janice I knew was mad enough to kill her now ex-husband. So, I made a couple of unnecessary stops along the way.

"Chica," she said, calling me by the nickname she'd given me. "You think you're slick. You stopped at the gas pump but the car's full. Then you stopped at the cigarette store, and neither of us smoke."

She was right. I couldn't take her home right then. I wanted my friend more than I wanted to come up with bail money.

Janice is now with the love of her life, a man who adores and appreciates her like no other male ever has. I call him "the jubilee husband," the one who came after nineteen plus years of emotional, mental, physical, and intimate famine.

Janine A. Ingram

Let me tell you about this woman. She is a powerful prayer warrior and can manifest abundance, prosperity, and opportunities like nobody's business! Our experience began on her journey to write *Born to be Rich*. Some people pray, but there are others who can put up that prayer that you know the Creator is sending down angels, guides, teachers … e'rebody to come help with that request. Janine taught me about not giving from an empty cup and filling yourself first, and that The Creator answers all prayers even if that answer is, "Not right now."

Transition: From Forgotten to Forgiven and Highly Favored

Jamyi Joy

This powerful woman survived a horrific ordeal within the walls of a penal institution that was further compounded by the legal drama when she was burned at the state. Yes, I meant state, not stake. Her courage and strength are legendary, and her support of me and the Tribe has been an amazing thing.

You Can Heal Your Life by Louise L. Hay, was the book Sesvalah recommended I read (use) while working on my healing journey, mostly because the content is a powerful exploration on how there is an affirmation for nearly every dis-ease and disease in the mind and body. That one book has been beneficial in my life in so many ways, in healing from physical abuse from my mother, sexual abuse from my father and uncle—and it has helped tremendously in helping me become healthy and complete.

But Louise's journey with this book has been the most amazing. She self-published because it was rejected by every major publishing house. Then, the book landed on the *New York Times* Bestseller's list for thirteen weeks. From there, she wrote other books that spoke to the power of positive thinking, visualization, and other techniques. After that, she started a publishing house and has published authors such as Wayne Dyer, Marianne Williamson, Deepak Chopra, Suz Orman, and so many others ...

When I finally met her at an I Can Do It conference and she was autographing my book, she looked at my name and said, "I recognize that name." I thought she might have, because I'd written to her legal department to use a quote from one of her books in one of mine. I told her, and she asked the title, and when I said, "It's Every Woman Needs a Wife," she then said, "I read that book." And she smiled.

I promise you that was the highlight of my life.

NK's Tribe Called Success is an amazing group of individuals, who provide their own set of lessons in taking care of my mental and physical well-being. Also, they continue to teach me about patience and compassion.

Everyone has a story to tell, and as a book coach and Book Whisperer, I'm one of the people who can help you tell it well. Healing from a traumatic past meant that part of my purpose is to help others tell their truth, their stories, and to share the ways they healed and survived things that were meant to take them out of the game before it even began.

Chapter 12

Merry Heart Centered Leadership

Working for various law firms over the years, I totally understand what it's like to be employed by people who don't lead from the heart. They lead from a position of power and ego. Honestly, it means sometimes they're not simply being—forgive my English—an asshole, they're actually a whole ass.

Money is the root of all evil. The verse is actually the love of money is the root of all evil. You need it to live on a daily basis, so money isn't bad. The not quite legit things people do to get it is another matter. When people are not living in integrity, living in lack and limitation of their thoughts, not realizing there is more than enough abundance for everyone, that is when power can dismantle a person from the inside out. Jim Rohn's quote impacted my life: If you work hard for someone else, you'll make a living. Work hard on yourself, and you'll make a fortune.

See, I've been playing fast and loose with my literary path as a book coach, publishing consultant, and book whisperer. I do it because I love helping people tell their life stories and the ones from their imagination, not because I sought to lean into it totally as a way to pay for my life. As a survivor of both physical and sexual abuse, I managed to turn the pain of my tragic beginnings into my passion, and put that passion onto the page. But now I'm ready to turn those pages into something that means doing what I love, and the abundance will be there.

If there's anyone reading this who's on the fence, move in wisdom. Create an exit plan from your day job that's done in ease, comfort, and joy. If nothing else, 2020 taught a lot of people to pivot away from depending so heavily on the resource and become more connected to The Source.

Raising your vibration, removing toxic people and manipulators from your life, understanding that abundance is unlimited and available to anyone and everyone, will gain you money and line your bank accounts. Power and respect may follow, but they aren't the focus for living your soul's purpose.

In my literary life, I lead from the heart, because in healing from my traumatic past, my heart is sometimes the best thing I have to give.

The Tribe has been the best road map for learning to lead from a heart-centered space. But the youngsters in my circle have also taught me a few lessons.

My hope for the future is that women will have more roles in making the laws around this camp. I never understood how there are more women on the planet, but we aren't in leadership roles that represent those numbers. We now see the importance of that. We've seen some powerful strides by women in politics, and I'd love to see even more.

Also, I want females to take more chances than ever before. It's been said that women going out for a position, make sure they check off all the boxes listing the qualifications for the position before applying. Men might only have half of those qualities, but will try anyway. I'd like to see more of that risk-taking from women to forge their path.

Recently, power play by two women let me know that they are truly doing it for themselves.

My niece, Leslie, went for a position and asked for a qualifying salary. They tried to low-ball her and said, "Well, we're a not for profit." And she replied, Yes, but I'm not a not for profit. I have to live." Well, what a way to say that. She turned down that position and accepted one that was willing to pay what she wanted, with benefits that worked for her.

My son's fiancé, Donisha, applied for a position, and they too offered her less than she asked, and truly expected her to accept it on the spot. She told them, "Let me think about it."

She didn't even make it home before they called her to offer the salary she quoted. My son and I were in the car to celebrate her win.

Her current boss, who recommended her for the position, said, "I knew that was going to come back to bite me in the ass." But I love that she wasn't pressured and would have walked away from that "opportunity" until something better came along.

My son is the one who taught me, and also shared with her, about valuing who you are and what you're worth. When I talked to him about lowering his prices for a particular group, he promptly told me, "Mom, I love you, but in business, I don't resent the work, and I don't want to resent the client."

Enough said. Shut me all the way down and made me reevaluate how I handle my consultations.

Though I worried about being a single mother and raising a man who could love, value, and appreciate the women in his life, a recent event warmed my heart. My son coordinated a surprise proposal for his girlfriend. They live in Houston, but both of them are from Chicago. To pull it off, he worked with her family and friends. He's been reading the book, *Act As If: The Secret Power of Your Thoughts* by Ehryck Gilmore, so he held to the thought of the proposal taking place in Chicago, in front of Buckingham fountain. It was their anniversary, and she wanted to go out of the country. So he saw that as a mountain, but with all the restrictions, she decided against it. He could breathe, and everything was on point for Chicago.

The weather leading up to the date alternated between sunny and gloomy, but rain was predicted for that particular day.

"It's not going to rain on my proposal, Mom."

Maybe you should move it to Navy Pier

"It's not going to rain on my proposal, Mom."

Called back and ... maybe we should move it to the restaurant

"It's not going to rain on my proposal, Mom."

The closer the time came for me to go downtown to Buckingham fountain, my heart pounded in my chest because the sky was still overcast, and the sun wasn't even thinking about coming out.

When I made it to the car and put my hand on the steering wheel, the first sign of fair weather greeted me. The sun peered from behind a cloud, and I texted him that I was on my way. He texted back, *we will see you there.*

Let me tell y'all, the sun came out and dried up everything and kept shining for the rest of the day. I should have believed him. Hooked up to tubes in the hospital recently, he had the hospital staff send me a picture of him with a prayer book and phone charger in his hand. He couldn't breathe, he couldn't move. But that image right there let me know he was going to be all right. But her words to him after he held out the ring and letters that they had written to each other the year before, spoke volumes about who he was to her.

Now I'm going to be honest, he tries that weather thing for

an outdoor wedding and I'm going to damn near pass out. But on that day, the weather was his mountain and he climbed it, went around it, and went through it.

These three have recently impacted me in a profound way, and they won't "amble through life" trying to figure things out for as long as I had to. I found my purpose purely by divine intervention. Writing was the medium I used. So leading from that place of being a survivor and not a victim is also leaning in to that part of my purpose in helping others tell their truth, their life stories, and how they triumphed over the situations that were designed to discourage and defeat them.

As a literary agent and book whisperer, I'm the founder of NK's Tribe Called Success— a group of forty-five authors, some of whom are *New York Times* bestsellers and *USA TODAY* bestsellers like myself. We support each other through marketing together and collaborating in series and anthologies. What sets us apart from other writers' groups is that we also provide the spiritual, emotional, and financial support that comes with being open and putting one's life on display.

Florenza Denise Lee, one of the Tribe members with a book in this series (*Purpose*), read this part of *Transition* and we had a wonderful discussion:

Some use God's word to justify slavery, domestic violence, imprisonment, and systematic racism rather than preach peace, joy, salvation, and love. The God who announced His plan of salvation to Eve by declaring, "your seed will crush the enemy's head, and the enemy will bruise your seed's heel," is the same who sent word of His Son's birth through an angel to a virgin named Mary. Christ valued women so much. He had His most profound conversations with women. Christ performed astounding miracles through them, and following his resurrection, He appeared to the women first.

Throughout scripture, God's love for women may be found, from Genesis to Revelation.

We've seen what happens in the world when people lead from anything but the heart. It causes heartache, confusion, and sadness. My Tribe and inner circle helps keep me grounded.

The Levites went in head first, then cycled back and told The Creator what they were going to do. Of course, disaster followed. Leading has everything to do with making sure what's in the heart is for the highest and best good of yourself and everyone involved.

This is Naleighna Kai, and I'm done writing ... for now.

Loving Me for Me by Naleighna Kai

Fourteen-year-old Reign was forced to get up in front of the church and apologize for shaming her mother by getting pregnant. She complied but was angry the entire time. Especially since she was fully aware of things going on behind the scenes. While she still held the microphone, she paused and then ended her apology with, "But I have a question, though. Is it only the girls you want to apologize just because you can see what we've done?" She rubbed her hand over her extended belly as the question drew murmurs of discontent. "Dawn got pregnant. No one asked Mason to come up here and apologize. Alexa got knocked up. No one made Eric say he was sorry. My brothers weren't made to get up here either."

The congregation roared with disapproval aimed directly at her. Some of them stood, raising their voices in contempt.

"Now, I know it does not excuse what I did," Reign continued, holding up a hand to signal they should quiet down because she wasn't done. "But I'm just saying Brother Harold's been sleeping with Sister Odessa's husband for the past two years. Everybody knows it." She focused on the golden man whose face turned a magnificent red. "Oh, and I don't see Sister Justine and Brother Martin up here apologizing for getting busy in the choir room during rehearsal when the pastor's wife caught 'em a few months ago."

"Now, wait a minute," Brother Martin stood, shaking his fist at Reign. His wife yanked him back down in the pew, then slapped her purse on top of his head nearly knocking him unconscious. Sister Justine left her husband's side and tried to run from the church. Her exit was blocked by the ushers who seemed to be having a grand old time with all of the skeletons creaking out of the closet and running up the church aisle as if the devil was on their heels. One of them, Sister Dorothy, even managed to give Reign the thumbs up sign, so she'd keep the party going.

"I'm just saying let's keep it fair," she said, ducking out of the reach of Deacon Jones who was making an attempt to snatch the microphone from her. "A sin's a sin. I think everybody should take a turn up here." She gestured toward Deacon Byrne as she slid up the aisle, managing to still be heard over all the chaos. "That is a *whole bottle* of Dr. Tichenor's in your pocket 'cause you need a little nip of that eighty-proof every now. Nobody needs fresh breath that bad." She winked at him, and even his wife laughed. "My mama told me that one."

The entire congregation was now on their feet, in heated conversations, some arguing about the truth she let spill. Choir members hastily left their seats. A few of them managed to tip out of the back door to the lower level before she let loose on them, too. The usher board had closed the rear doors so no one could run out that way. One of them sprinted down the right side aisle to get to the choir entrance to block that as well.

Reign slid a sly look to her fuming mother, who was dressed in the pristine white uniform of the pastor's personal nurse and was sitting in a special seat near the pulpit. "And the only reason my mother's on the nurse's board," Reign said, keeping a steely glare on her mother. "Taking care of the pastor, getting his water and handkerchiefs, fixing all that good food and baking those sweet potato pies especially for him, is 'cause she's hoping for a little ... *sin* of her own."

"I knew it," the First Lady said, waggling a finger at Thelma, wide brim hat tipping almost off her head. She nearly climbed over the pew, aiming to get to Reign's mother. Two women nearest her, held the stout woman back.

Reign looked toward the red-faced Pastor who was fit to be tied. "And doesn't look like he's turning down nothing but his collar, so maybe I should pass the mic to him. Come to think of it, Brother Jimmy, Brother Patrick, and Brother Russell need some time up here, too." She moved up the middle aisle and back toward the pulpit ignoring the three men in question. "Each one of them offered me some money—for the baby's sake. That's what they said. But they wanted a *little something* in return. They seemed really happy that I was pregnant 'cause that meant I couldn't get knocked up again." She swept a gaze across the congregation as Sister Delores yanked the microphone from her hand. Reign dashed toward the choir stand to snatch another one from where the organist played. "And they're not the only ones up in here who did that. I've got nine offers from church men alone and close to $9,536.50." She waggled an index finger. "And don't forget the fifty cents. That's a lot of dough, especially for a sinner like me." She shrugged as if she hadn't set the church on holy fire. "So let's be fair about this sin thing."

"That's enough, young lady," the pastor said from the pulpit, gesturing for someone to grab her. Reign faked left, then moved until she was in the far left aisle blocked in by a few folks who were grinning at her efforts and didn't let the deacons near her.

"Oh, so I'm a *young lady* now?" Reign shot back, glowering angrily at him. "When you told my mother that she needed to bring her *little whore* before the church to apologize."

"No he didn't," Sister Mabel shouted.

"But you didn't make your nieces get up here when *they* got pregnant. Or any of the boys right here in this church who made them that way. I count about twelve so far. And that's not including the ones who had abortions." Reign snapped her fingers as realization hit. "But wait a minute, that counts as sin, too, right? But it's not one that you can see."

Gasps echoed throughout the congregation.

"So which is it? Whore or young lady?" she taunted, stretching out her hands as if in supplication. "Either way, I'm just saying—a sin is a sin. Let the church say 'Amen'."

Get your copy of *Loving Me for Me* wherever books are sold.

My Time in the Sun by Naleighna Kai

Chicago, Illinois
Twelve years later

"The first lady was a prostitute," Terrence Henderson bellowed loud enough to carry the entire length of the church sanctuary and echo from the cathedral ceilings.

All eyes were focused on the richly-dressed minister swaggering past the organ, down the plush maroon carpet of the center aisle, then around the maple wood pews filled with morning worshippers.

"A fourteen-year-old prostitute," he continued. "Not the kind of woman we want our little girls and young women to emulate."

Aridell Henderson Slaughter stood, joined by several other members of the Mothers Board, as she said, "Get thee behind me Satan. And *stay* there."

Sam, the choir director, shouted, "Have you lost your cotton-picking, chicken-plucking mind, mother—" he caught himself before adding the last, more profane part of that Southern saying. "How dare you put her on blast like that."

The silence was nothing short of mind-blowing. Slowly, murmurs became whispers. Those whispers became a collective voice. That collective voice became a roar of discontent so loud it could have broken the stained-glass window of Christ holding out the goblet of wine to Mary Magdalene.

Kari Baltimore's heart rate sped up to the point where that life-sustaining organ nearly burst from her chest. She brushed a hand down her thighs to smooth the lavender silk dress that draped her curvaceous frame. She glanced at her husband in the pulpit, noticing the second he quickly shuttered his shock as he stood and moved to the edge of the dais.

Pastor Tony Baltimore's hand went up. Voices trickled back down to whispers, then silence slowly descended once again.

"And you're saying this in front of the entire congregation hoping to achieve what, Minister Henderson?" Tony challenged, his sun-kissed complexion aflame with angry color. "To somehow make me ashamed of my wife? To make the members turn against her?"

For a second, the confidence that had been so evident in Terrence's arrogant demeanor slipped. But only for a second. Because the church's board and deacons suddenly rounded him in what seemed to be a show of support.

Kari zeroed in on their solemn expressions which didn't show one ounce of surprise. Evidently, this outburst was a long time in the making.

The fire in Tony's dark brown eyes would normally be enough to quell the most disruptive of people. But not Terrence Henderson. Ever since he'd been ordained to preach by some still-yet-to-be-identified pastor in California where he once lived, the ambitious minister had his sights on being the pastor of the church founded by his great-great grandfather, the good Reverend Jacob Lee Henderson. The position of pastor had been held for four generations of Henderson men. That is, until a scandal with one of the members forced Terrence Henderson's father to make an exit stage left—with teenage mistress in tow—long before the son of his wife had come of age to enter the pulpit.

A board of deacons and trustees had conducted a series of interviews and background checks, searching for a new pastor to lead the modest congregation. Overlooking a slightly flawed past, they'd deemed Anthony "Tony" J. Baltimore worthy to make the cut. If Kari had undergone the same rigorous scrutiny, they might have seen that she had a little baggage *and* a carry-on.

Tony pinned his focus on Terrence, his shoulders tense with conviction as he said, "This woman is not just my wife, she's my partner in helping people in this community find the God they stopped serving a long time ago. She's a spiritual ambassador who helps people find peace when there's so little of it in other aspects of their lives." Admidst a round of Amen's, he moved down the aisle until he was toe-to-toe with Terrence, towering over him by a few inches. "And you couldn't even come at me in a way that was decent and in order, like a board meeting. No, you took the coward's way and tried to shame her publicly in the middle of Sunday morning service."

The members—from the choir, musicians, all the way to the usher board—were on their feet, some voicing their support of Tony, but a surprising number of them siding with Terrence. A good majority of the rest of them stayed silent watching the fireworks as though they couldn't believe something this scandalous would unfold in Sunday service right between prayer and scripture.

"And the first lady hasn't stood up to say it isn't true," Terrence challenged with a haughty lift of his chin.

"That's because her husband's defending her honor and her character," Sister Terry interjected. "And she's doing what a first lady should do—she's letting him."

Several choruses of "Amen" and "that's right, my sister", "you'd better say that" rang through the sanctuary.

The one thing Kari feared most was playing out right before her eyes, hurting the man she loved in a way she never wanted. At that moment, she wished she could vanish into thin air as Enoch had when he went to be with the Lord. No natural death there. One minute he was, and then he wasn't.

The hard part about all this? Her husband didn't know anything about this fragment of her past. She had buried it so deep, even she couldn't remember the details. That was supposed to be a good thing. Fresh start. New life.

How sad that one man's ambition could serve as another woman's destruction.

Get your copy of *My Time in the Sun* wherever books are sold.

King of Devon by Naleighna Kai

"What do you mean she's in labor? Jai gripped the edge of the desk, with the phone pressed to his ear. "That's ... well, that's impossible."

His heart slammed in his chest when Kelly Peterson didn't retract her statement.

Everything was happening much faster than he expected. A patient, who fell into a coma after a tragic car accident, had been in his health center for a year. Her circumstances took a downward and unfortunate turn because she had not been pregnant when she arrived. He, along with all of his male employees, were now under intense investigation. Didn't help matters any that almost all of the employees were ex-felons who were aiming for a second chance in life. Even worse, his holistic practices at Chetan had drawn the ire of the medical industry because of the substantial success rate. The Health Bureau had been trying to find any reason to shut him down. Temple Devaughn's newborn baby would provide a direct avenue for that to happen.

The media was abuzz over the situation and their actions were being fueled by Donald Amos, a former high-level member of The Castle who was itching to regain his seat on the board. Not going to happen with Jai and his eight fellow

Kings at the helm. Dr. Taylor had said Temple would carry to term. Seven, almost eight months in and evidently, nature had other plans. His life was about to hit the porcelain goddess and circle the bowl for a few rounds before the royal flush. "In labor, right now?"

"Yes," Kelly whispered. "Right now."

He rounded the glass desk and grabbed a leather briefcase, then jammed the meeting notes he'd been scanning inside. "Are the paramedics on their way?"

"They're about twenty minutes out," she replied, and he steeled himself for even more bad news. "Dr. Taylor is in Africa on a health mission, and isn't expected back until next week. So, no one from her team is at the hospital right now. That means whoever is going to be part of the delivery hasn't been briefed on the delicacy of this particular situation. Overall, things are about to be pretty damn interesting."

And that would present a problem within itself. Jai had chosen Dr. Julie Taylor because she was not afraid of the challenges Temple's pregnancy presented. Every other doctor had taken a hard pass. Their careers were on the line, and the potential failure could damage their reputations and their licenses. Julie had been a family practitioner who changed her discipline once she realized how few OB/GYNs were in Africa, and how desperately they were needed.

"I'm on my way," he said to Kelly as he made it to the front door of his home. "Thanks for all you do."

"It's always a pleasure, Jai."

Twelve minutes later, he arrived at the glass-and-steel building that housed the Chetan Healing Center and parked in his reserved spot near the entrance. This frantic pace wasn't a good way to start the morning, but the situation called for him to be on high alert.

The moment the smoke-tinted doors slid open and he set foot across the threshold—all while balancing his phone, tablet, and briefcase—Kelly rushed toward him. Her ivory skin was flushed to crimson and her reddish-brown hair plastered to the side of her face as though she'd sprinted an entire marathon. Not a good sign.

"We can't reach Temple's mother or fiancé," she said, gasping for breath. "The center has power of attorney for health care. You'll have to act on our patient's behalf."

A chill passed through Jai, rendering him almost numb. He handed off his briefcase and accepted the documents she held as he tried to come to terms with what her words meant. "Power of attorney for an issue that happened at Chetan, yes. This is something entirely different."

"No, it isn't," she countered, hooking her arm under his and directing him to where the paramedics were wheeling a gurney across the threshold toward the waiting ambulance. "Go with her to the hospital."

"Hey, be gentle," he warned the crew navigating the concrete. "She's not a piece of meat."

The men didn't stop or bat an eye. "She's comatose," the slimmer one of the pair said. "She can't feel it anyway."

"That is *not* acceptable," Jai roared, and Kelly held his arm in a vice-like grip to keep him in place. "What if she was your mother . . . or sister? Treat. Her. Gently."

Kelly relaxed her hold on him, and Jai threw her a glance, expressing his thanks without speaking. She nodded in response and gave him a slight smile.

The men halted a few feet from the vehicle, shared a speaking glance that revealed their irritation, but they complied by significantly slowing their movements.

Jai stepped into the back of the ambulance and perched on a silver bench, watching as they situated the IV, then strapped the patient in before the burly one ran to the front and sped away from the sidewalk.

The fifteen-minute drive was tense and silent, except for the blare of the siren and the furtive glances the two-member crew sent his way—one from the rearview mirror. The ambulance pulled into the emergency bay of Meridian Hospital. A team of nurses and a salt-and-pepper haired doctor with a dour expression swept out of the doors and scurried toward the vehicle.

He extended a hand to Jai. "I'm Dr. Christian."

When the two nurses gripped the silver railings, the shorter of the paramedics said, "Treat her like glass or this guy will have a conniption."

His partner nodded in Jai's direction and scowled.

"That was uncalled for," Dr. Christian said, his tone sharp and forbidding, matching the frown that appeared on his face.

"We don't have the time to belabor the point that comatose doesn't mean deceased," Jai shot back, glaring at the two men who were ignoring the warning looks from the nurses.

Dr. Christian flinched, then his head whipped around to Jai. "Wait a minute. Did you say comatose?"

Jai kept his gaze on the men and didn't bother to answer the question.

The doctor recovered his composure and gave the two emergency personnel a stern look as he warned, "You'll hear about this later."

"Whatever, man." The stockier one waved him off.

Jai made a mental note to address the entire situation when things calmed down. No telling what other process those two had let slide. While he understood that most of their fellow paramedics had been on strike for a while, their attitude was out of order.

The preparation for the baby's arrival soon became a synchronicity of nurses pulling together all needed materials, equipment, and getting Jai in place. The fact that the doctor had been thrown for a loop became evident in the furrowed brow, anxious expression, and solemn bearing.

"You're the father?" Dr. Christian asked, suiting up and gesturing for Nurse Jennifer to outfit Jai in the same manner.

"No, I have power of attorney to see to Temple's well-being."

Dr. Christian lowered his mask to ask, "So, she was pregnant when she arrived at your center?"

"The notes are all here, doctor," Jai said, passing him a set of documents Kelly had the presence of mind to compile and place in a manila folder.

The doctor slipped off his gloves, scanned the pages, then blinked several times before focusing on Jai. "She's *that* woman? From the news?"

"Yes," Jai answered through his teeth and offered nothing more since the rest of the nursing staff had turned curious gazes in their direction.

Dr. Christian held up a hand to keep Jai from moving forward. "So, we're going to do a C-section to get this over and done with."

"Dr. Taylor already had a plan in place to induce a semi-natural labor," Jai said, flipping the page and putting an index finger on the summary paragraph of the health plan he'd worked out with Dr. Taylor. Her method would be best for Temple's overall health."

"That might be true," he countered, switching out his gloves. "But I'm not Dr. Taylor and what I say in this hospital goes."

"I get that," Jai shot back, moving until only a few feet stood between them. "And I'm still saying, do not cut her unless it's absolutely necessary. You haven't even assessed her to see what the best course should be."

Jai had researched several cases that were similar to Temple's in that the women were also pregnant and in a coma. The difference had been in the fact that in the information he came across, the women were already pregnant before going into the coma. Temple's pregnancy occurred several months *after* she arrived at Chetan. The plan Dr. Taylor put in place meant a possible chance for Temple to fully recover after the birth and resume treatment at Chetan. She'd need special care, and he along with his staff, were well prepared for that contingency.

The nurses were now tending to Temple, but moving at such a slow pace Jai was certain they were listening intently to the exchange.

"Dr. Taylor is willing to take chances that I am not," he admitted. "It's my license and practice that would be at stake, not hers. The patient isn't having a normal delivery process and that bears a great deal of consideration. It's possible she would not survive. Be more merciful that way."

"And your attitude is the very thing I'd hoped to avoid. She's been through enough," Jai said, giving the people gathered around them a cursory glance. "Having to go through a C-Section would be unnecessarily traumatic."

"No more traumatic than what happened to put her in this condition," Dr. Christian shot back, gesturing to Temple's belly. "And it happened in your special little facility. I don't even know why you're here. Aren't you under investigation as one of the men who might have impregnated her?"

Jaidev Maharaj saw red.

Get your copy of *King of Devon* wherever books are sold.

King of Durabia by Naleighna Kai

No good deed goes unpunished, or that's how Ellena Kiley feels after she rescues a child and the former Crown Prince of Durabia offers to marry her.

Kamran learns of a nefarious plot to undermine his position with the Sheikh and jeopardize his ascent to the throne. He's unsure how Ellena, the fiery American seductress, fits into the plan but she's a secret weapon he's unwilling to relinquish.

Ellena is considered a sister by the Kings of the Castle and her connection to Kamran challenges her ideals, her freedoms, and her heart. Plus, loving him makes her a potential target for his enemies. When Ellena is kidnapped, Kamran is forced to bring in the Kings.

In the race against time to rescue his woman and defeat his enemies, the kingdom of Durabia will never be the same.

Chapter 1

"You risked your life for my grandson," Sheikh Aayan said, his voice echoing through the ornate throne room. "Ask for anything and I will see what can be done."

Ellena scanned the expectant faces of the throngs of people who had gathered for this unexpected audience with the ruler of Durabia. Most of their tunics and dishdashas differed from her casual attire of a simple white blouse and black slacks. "Thank you, but that isn't necessary. I did what anyone would do."

"Evidently, not everyone," he said, and his angry glare focused on the bodyguard, caregivers, and everyone who had stood by when Javed, the little royal, had swept past Ellena and landed on the moving conveyor belt.

All of them had frozen in place the moment Javed brushed against the rubber bounding strip and was sucked into the void. The video of Ellena dropping her tote bag, diving in after him, and cradling him in her arms as they were both tossed through the maze of steel and vinyl, all while being battered by suitcases and duffel bags alike, went viral.

Ellena had closed her eyes, bracing under each blow. Javed's laughter was a stark contrast to her pain. The cameras caught everything, including the tail end of the journey when Ellena tumbled out of the final drop onto another belt and finally into the metal cart that would carry the luggage onto the plane. Security finally found their legs and scrambled to make it to Ellena and the little boy before they sustained further injuries. Well, before she did. Her fleshy body was all the protection that Javed needed.

Javed Khan, a great grandson of the royal family, was completely unharmed. Ellena, on the day of arrival for a class reunion vacation, had to be rushed to the hospital. They kept her overnight. She sustained a few cuts and bruises that matched the dent in her ego when the entire world saw her tossed head over ass multiple times. And when the adrenaline wore off and the fear kicked in, the little royal refused to let her go. He even had to travel in the emergency transport with her because none of the guards or caregivers managed to force him to release his hold on Ellena.

Now she stood in a palace situated in the heart of a metropolis in the Middle East with a décor that was unrivaled by anything she'd ever seen. Gold—everything was layered with it—the walls, doors, accented by purples and reds that added a sultry warmth to all of the opulence of the furniture, paintings, and draperies covering massive windows.

"Well, to be honest, I haven't wanted much," she said with a nervous laugh. "And the only thing I don't have is a husband. But I'd love to have a place here in Durabia, where I can come and go as I please. If that is at all possible."

"Done," the Sheikh said, beckoning to the man who had visited the hospital twice to see about her condition. "Kamran, come."

"Wait. What?" She laughed and rested a hand on her ample bosom. "An apartment, really?"

"Your new husband," he answered with a grand gesture that would have made Vanna White proud. "This is my oldest son."

The man was drop-dead gorgeous. Olive complexion, dark hair, goatee neatly trimmed to perfection, and piercing brown eyes that missed nothing. He was more suited to a fashion runway than a palace. Truthfully, she wasn't sure if it was the tunics, neat beards, head coverings or what. Durabia seemed to have no shortage of handsome men. But the Sheikh's son was a masterpiece, exuding the kind of confidence that came with a man who was certain of his place in the world. His gaze swept across her face with a complexion slightly darker than his olive tone, then quickly covered the distance over her curves, then his lips lifted in a warm, appreciative smile that practically lit up his dark brown eyes and sent heat straight to places that had been dormant since the Queen of Sheba caused King Solomon to lose his entire mind.

Ellena shook her head, clearing her mind of all manner of wickedness that came after that wonderful assessment. "I think you misunderstood. I was joking about the husband part. The apartment, time share or whatever you call them here, that's all I really want."

"You will have both," the Sheikh commanded with a nod of finality no one would dare to question. "A husband and a place here. My son needs a wife and you mentioned you do not have a husband. Problem solved."

"But doesn't he have to give you heirs or something?" She instinctively brought her hands near her belly. "My eggs are old enough to be married and have children of their own by now."

First, a roar of laughter went up from him. A few moments later, it was mirrored by everyone standing around her. Yes, that line was funny, but the one thing she understood was the unfairness of the situation. At least for Kamran. And that was no laughing matter.

The Sheikh waved away that thought. "That will not be a concern. He is unable to give you or any woman children. And a woman of African descent will never sit on the Durabian throne. We are safe on that score."

A shadow of sadness flickered in Kamran's eyes and his skin flushed a shade darker. Ellena tried to read a deeper meaning into his father's words. She still came up with *unfair*. "So, you just throw him to a random woman because he can't give you an heir? He is *still* a man. He *still* has value," she insisted. "A brain, intelligence, and a purpose." She inhaled, trying to tamp down on her anger. "The apartment is fine, Sheikh. Thank you, but I will not be foisted on a man who has no say in the matter. That's downright cruel."

A gasp came from the core of people around them before silence descended in the room. Even Kamran flinched.

The Sheikh's face darkened with anger as he slowly came to his feet. "Are you refusing—"

"Give me nine days—"

All eyes focused on the handsome man, who left his father's side and moseyed toward her like some type of Arabian cowboy. All swagger, no gun necessary.

"Give me nine days," he repeated and moved across the expensive Persian carpet until he stood in front of her, towering over her near six-foot height by three inches of his own. "Nine days for me to show you Durabia, to answer any questions you may have. To let you explore the place, the people, the culture. Then you decide."

Ellena found it hard to catch her breath. The man was so virile she felt warm all the way to her follicles. "Nine days? I have to go home. I have a job back there. I used all of my vacation and two of my sick days for this trip."

"Your job?" he asked, frowning as though he couldn't fathom what the word meant.

"Yes. A job. Nine to five. Benefits. All of that. You know, what regular folks do to keep an address."

Kamran remained silent for a few moments as he peered at her. "How much do they pay you?"

She winced, then flickered a gaze to his right and felt the intensity of everyone's attention. "It doesn't matter."

"How much?" He beckoned for her to come nearer. "Whisper it to me."

Ellena hesitated a moment, then complied, moving so close she inhaled the intoxicating scent of sandalwood. She managed to whisper an answer, then inched back to put a little distance between them.

"For the rest of your life?" he asked, his tone and wide eyes reflecting the incredulity registered in his facial expression.

"Until I'm sixty-seven and retire," she replied, daunted by his tone. "But there's also health benefits and other factors that I can't put a number on."

Kamran blinked as though doing a set of mental calculations and coming up with what probably amounted to simple interest on his bank account. "Give me the particulars and I will wire the money into your account."

She parted her lips to protest but he held up a hand. "Saying yes to taking me as your husband is still your choice. With this, I am simply ensuring your peace of mind. And as a gift for your kindness, your selflessness in saving a child who was a stranger to you."

Ellena let out a long, slow breath, because staying here permanently, marrying him, would be a lost cause. She loved her job as a personal assistant at Vantage Point. Alejandro Reyes, a "Fixer" of everything from political and corporate espionage, to terrorist attacks, was the absolute best person to work for. And she loved the predictability of her life. Traveling overseas was the most adventurous event in her life. Still, curiosity won out over common sense and she said, "All right. Thank you."

"Now we go about the business of getting to know one another," he said, smiling as though her consent brought him much pleasure. Evidently, he wanted this to happen and the intensity of his gaze bore into her soul. "So that you can make an informed decision, yes?"

She glanced over his shoulder, taking in some of the envious looks a few of the women tried to hide. "Why are you doing this?" she asked him. "Why are you allowing them to serve you up to some foreign woman as if you do not have value?"

"Because I recognize this is God's will," he answered. "And who am I to leave a precious gift unwrapped?"

Her eyebrows drew in, as she tried to decipher the hidden meaning behind his words. The man had a peaceful, confident air but also a playful vibe about him.

"Yes, that was a double entendre." His smile widened and she could swear the heavens opened up and smiled with him.

Good Lord, I'm in trouble.

Get your copy of *King of Durabia* wherever books are sold.

About the Author

Naleighna Kai is the *USA TODAY*, *Essence®* national bestselling and award-winning author of several women's fiction, contemporary fiction, Christian fiction, Romance, erotica, and science fiction novels that plumb the depth of unique relationships and women's issues. She is also a contributor to a *New York Times* bestseller, one of AALBC's 100 Top Authors, a member of CVS Hall of Fame, Mercedes Benz Mentor Award Nominee, and the E. Lynn Harris Author of Distinction.

In addition to successfully cracking the code of landing a deal for herself and others with a major publishing house, she continues to "pay it forward" by organizing the annual Cavalcade of Authors and NK's Tribe Called Success which gives readers intimate access to the most accomplished writing talent today. She also serves as CEO of The Macro Group, LLC which offers aspiring and established authors assistance with ghostwriting, developmental editing, publishing, marketing, and other services to jump-start or enhance their writing careers.

www.naleighnakai.com

FB: @naleighnakai
IG: @naleighnakai
TW: @naleighnakai

The Merry Hearts Inspirational Series will warm your heart and touch your soul . . .

www.ingramcontent.com/pod-product-compliance
Lightning Source LLC
Chambersburg PA
CBHW011802040426
42449CB00017B/3470